WORLD RELIGIONS
BUDDHISM
FOURTH EDITION

WORLD RELIGIONS

African Traditional Religion
Baha'i Faith
Buddhism
Catholicism & Orthodox Christianity
Confucianism
Daoism
Hinduism
Islam
Judaism
Native American Religions
Protestantism
Shinto
Sikhism
Zoroastrianism

WORLD RELIGIONS
BUDDHISM
FOURTH EDITION

by
Madhu Bazaz Wangu
Series Editors: Joanne O'Brien and Martin Palmer

CHELSEA HOUSE
PUBLISHERS
An imprint of Infobase Publishing

Chelsea House
An imprint of Infobase Publishing
132 West 31st Street
New York NY 10001

Library of Congress Cataloging-in-Publication Data
Wangu, Madhu Bazaz.
 Buddhism / by Madhu Bazaz Wangu.—4th ed.
   p. cm. — (World religions)
 Previously published: New York : Facts On File, 2006.
 Includes bibliographical references and index.
 ISBN 978-1-60413-105-5
 1. Buddhism—Juvenile literataure. I. Title. II. Series.

 BQ4032.W36 2009
 294.3—dc22

      2008051265

Chelsea House books are available at special discounts when purchased in bulk quantities for businesses, associations, institutions, or sales promotions. Please call our Special Sales Department in New York at (212) 967-8800 or (800) 322-8755.

You can find Chelsea House on the World Wide Web at http://www.chelseahouse.com

This book was produced for Chelsea House by Bender Richardson White, Uxbridge, U.K.
Project Editor: Lionel Bender
Text Editor: Ronne Randall
Designer: Ben White
Picture Researchers: Joanne O'Brien and Kim Richardson
Maps and symbols: Stefan Chabluk

Printed in China

CP BRW 10 9 8 7 6 5 4 3 2 1

This book is printed on acid-free paper.

All links and Web addresses were checked and verified to be correct at the time of publication. Because of the dynamic nature of the Web, some addresses and links may have changed since publication and may no longer be valid.

CONTENTS

PREFACE

Almost from the start of civilization, more than 10,000 years ago, religion has shaped human history. Today more than half the world's population practice a major religion or indigenous spiritual tradition. In many 21st-century societies, including the United States, religion still shapes people's lives and plays a key role in politics and culture. And in societies throughout the world increasing ethnic and cultural diversity has led to a variety of religions being practiced side by side. This makes it vital that we understand as much as we can about the world's religions.

The World Religions series, of which this book is a part, sets out to achieve this aim. It is written and designed to appeal to both students and general readers. The books offer clear, accessible overviews of the major religious traditions and institutions of our time. Each volume in the series describes where a particular religion is practiced, its origins and history, its central beliefs and important rituals, and its contributions to world civilization. Carefully chosen photographs complement the text, and sidebars, a map, fact file, glossary, bibliography, and index are included to help readers gain a more complete understanding of the subject at hand.

These books will help clarify what religion is all about and reveal both the similarities and differences in the great spiritual traditions practiced around the world today.

Buddhists as a Proportion of the Population.

50%–95%

2%–49%

0.1%–1.9%

Less than 0.1%

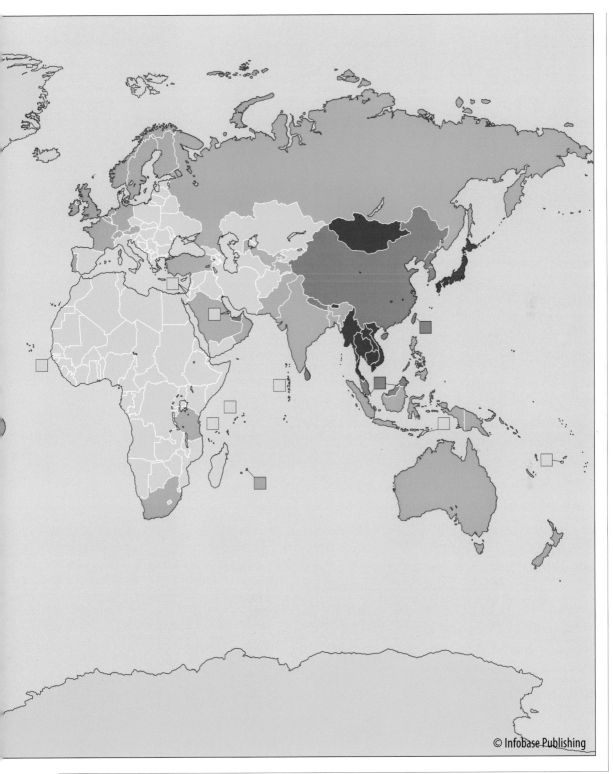

© Infobase Publishing

CHAPTER 1

INTRODUCTION: THE MODERN BUDDHIST WORLD

Approximately 370 million people in the world today are practicing Buddhists, making Buddhism the fourth largest of the world's religions. However, Buddhism has an influence even greater than the number of its adherents would indicate. From the time that Siddhartha Gautama—known as the Buddha—first preached his simple doctrine about 2,500 years ago, Buddhism has spread throughout Asia from its homeland in India. It has had a significant and lasting impact on India, China, Japan, Korea, Thailand, Mongolia, and other Asian nations.

Today Buddhism is the majority religion in Thailand, Mongolia, Cambodia, Myanmar (formerly Burma), Bhutan, Sri Lanka, Tibet, Laos, Vietnam, Japan, Taiwan, and Singapore. Though the most populous nation in the world, China, is officially atheist, a sizable minority of its people adhere to Buddhist beliefs. Millions more Chinese, though they are not practicing Buddhists, are influenced by the cultural aspects of Buddhism.

Buddhism is not confined solely to Asia. In the past century it has won admirers and followers in Europe and the United States.

A young Burmese monk in a temple shrine room. The gilt statues of the Buddha depict him with one hand touching the earth to symbolize enlightenment.

Indeed, the majority of the people in one U.S. state—Hawaii—is Buddhist.

All the countries that came under the influence of Buddhism were enriched culturally and artistically. The image of the Buddha appears in colossal statues, delicate figurines, and innumerable styles of art throughout Asia. Scenes from the Buddha's life are as important in Asian art as the story of Jesus Christ is in Western art.

WHAT IS BUDDHISM?

Buddhism is a path to spiritual discovery. Its founder, Siddhartha Gautama, looked at the human condition much as a doctor does. He found disease, decay, and death. He fully realized that joy and pleasure existed as well, but he recognized that those qualities did not last. All things in life were transient or temporary. So even in joy the awareness of impermanence and death caused unhappiness and suffering.

Because of his Indian background Siddhartha did not believe that death was a final release from suffering. In Indian religious tradition souls are reborn into new bodies after death. The cycle of birth, death, and rebirth goes on unendingly. All living beings are caught in this cycle. Siddhartha strove to find a way to get off the treadmill of endless rebirths. Through meditation he realized the path to final release and became enlightened.

THE EIGHTFOLD PATH

The Buddha diagnosed human desire in all its forms as the cause of suffering. Therefore his "treatment," or solution, was to eliminate desire by "right thoughts and right actions." This could be done by following the Eightfold Path. This was a series of eight stages of a high ethical code. The first stages on this path were guides, calling for kindly behavior to all living

The Awakened

Siddhartha Gautama devoted his life to pondering the problem of the never-ending cycle of birth, death, and rebirth. After living a life of luxury as a prince, he practiced self-denial. In the end neither provided the answers. Only through meditation did he reach an answer. In the moment of his insight he became the Buddha, a title that means "the enlightened" or "the awakened."

things. Later stages were more difficult and required meditation and discipline.

This truth, or law, of Buddhism is known as dharma. Indeed, Buddha dharma is the name of the religion in Asia. It is also called "the Middle Way." The Buddha advised those who wished to follow the dharma to avoid extremes of behavior, such as severe self-denial or, at the other extreme, selfish attachment to pleasure.

The Sangha

During his lifetime the Buddha institutionalized his teachings by forming the sangha. The sangha is the community of monks and nuns who practice the religion and teach it to others. Today the members of the sangha provide a living link with their religion's founder.

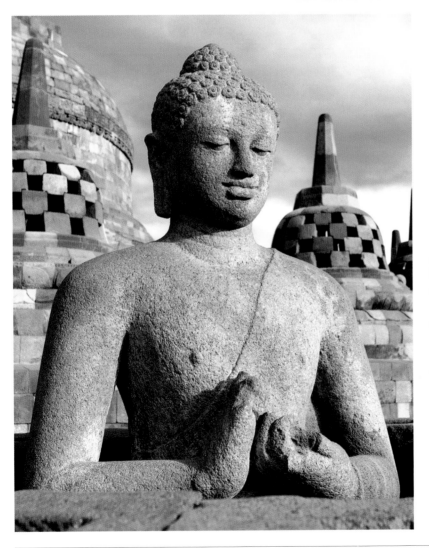

A stone carving of the Buddha on the huge stupa, or dome-shaped shrine, at Borobadur on the island of Java in Indonesia. The position of the Buddha's hands shows that he is teaching the dharma, the law and the way. The Buddha's hair is in a topknot, representing spiritual wisdom, and he has elongated earlobes, signifying his previous life of wealth when heavy jewels would have weighed down his ears.

He stated, "Avoid these two extremes: attachment to the pleasures of the senses, which is low and vulgar, and attachment to self-mortification, which is painful. Both are unprofitable."

NIRVANA

Correctly following the Eightfold Path brings one in time to nirvana, a term that is difficult to define. Buddhists have said that it cannot be described in words. It is not the heaven of Christianity or Islam. In Sanskrit, the ancient Indian language, *nirvana* means "blowing out" (as a flame is blown out). In Buddhism what is blown out is hatred, greed, and delusion.

Looking at it in another way, nirvana is the loss of the "ego," or "I" self, a condition that ends the path of suffering and pain when human beings travel from one life to another. The word *nirvana*

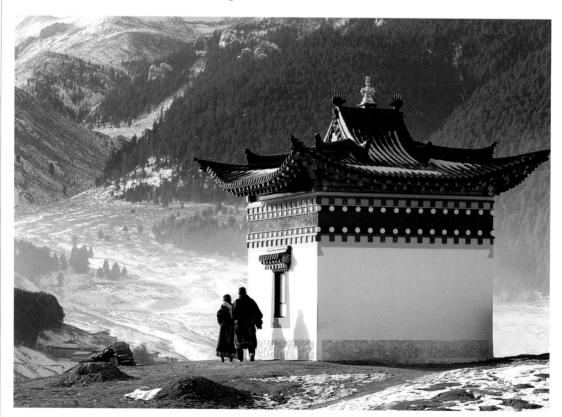

Pilgrims in Tibet entering a hilltop Buddhist temple for morning devotions.

also implies "boundless expansion," which may be described as becoming part of the universe. It was nirvana that Siddhartha attained when he became the Buddha.

AN ETHICAL CODE

Buddhism is like other religions in its concern for the welfare of humankind—indeed, for all living things. In the striving for the attainment of nirvana, it teaches a high ethical code. It asks its followers to abstain from taking life of any kind; not to lie, cheat, or steal; and to treat others with kindness. "Hatred does not cease by hatred at any time," said the Buddha. "Hatred ceases by love."

> ### Self-possession
>
> *Only a man himself can be the master of himself: who else from outside could be his master? When the Master and servant are one, then there is true help and self-possession.*
>
> —From the *Dhammapada* (12:160)

THE GREAT VARIETY OF BUDDHISM

The Buddha never wrote down his teachings. His disciples memorized his words, and their followers carried on the oral tradition. The first comprehensive written record of the Buddha's doctrine was not compiled until 500 years after his death.

THERAVADA AND MAHAYANA

By that time Buddhism had already developed two major forms: Theravada Buddhism and Mahayana Buddhism. In general Theravada's adherents followed more literally the teachings of the historic Buddha, while the followers of Mahayana more freely adapted the Buddha's doctrine.

By and large Theravada Buddhism is followed today by people on the southern rim of Asia—Sri Lanka, Myanmar, Thailand, Cambodia, Laos, and parts of Malaysia. Mahayana Buddhism spread north and east from India into China, Tibet, Vietnam, Korea, and Japan.

> ### OLDER RELIGIONS
>
> In many parts of Asia, Buddhism absorbed or provided a space for the continuation of older traditional religions such as Bon in Tibet. In other countries rivalry sometimes meant that the older religions redefined themselves against Buddhism. In China, for example, the rise of Buddhism led to the traditional religion of Daoism developing monasticism for the first time.

Missionaries from China spread Buddhism to Korea and from there it came to Japan. The Japanese, showing their ingenious talent for turning foreign things into uniquely Japanese traditions, assimilated Buddhism into their culture. Most Japanese today follow the practices of both Buddhism and Shinto, the ancient Japanese belief in *kami,* or nature spirits.

VARIETY OF PRACTICE

As a result of its tolerant tradition Buddhism today displays a wide variety of practices and customs. In Thailand, during the rainy season that begins in July, schoolchildren make candles to present as gifts to the local Buddhist temple and celebrate with song and dance. Each year in Sri Lanka orange-robed Buddhist monks lead an elephant through the streets. It carries one of the country's holiest Buddhist relics—a tooth of the Buddha himself. In Tibet spiritual guides called lamas gather around people who are dying, reciting certain texts to assist the dying person to reach a higher plane of existence. In Korea each April shops and houses are festooned with paper lanterns as colorful processions pass through the streets in celebration of the Buddha's birthday. In Japan many people simply recite the phrase "I call on the Amida Buddha" in their everyday lives. All these people are paying homage to the Buddha.

A MORAL MESSAGE

The message of Buddhism has an appeal on many different intellectual levels. It can be either very simple or immensely complicated. For the person with such everyday concerns as how to earn a living, it offers a moral message of compassion, honesty, and self-control. Its appeal is as great to a practitioner in industrial Japan as it is to peasants in rural communities of Southeast Asia. On the other hand it can provide a basis for lifelong meditation and thought.

Today, members of the sangha still teach and pursue the goal of enlightenment. Men and women put on the robes of Buddhist monks or nuns and enter monasteries. They spend much of their time reciting together the scriptures of Buddhism, or in solitary meditation on the truths of the religion. They depend on the donations of the faithful for their subsistence. Some take their alms bowls into the streets, and others receive donations of food or money at the monastery.

THE MONASTIC LIFE

Like Buddhism itself, the life of a monk or nun is flexible. Some people enter as children and stay for their entire lifetimes. Others lead the monastic life for a short time and then return to the everyday world. This is not frowned upon, for they have earned merit for the time they spent in complete devotion to the Buddhist way. In the countries of Southeast Asia it is very common for laypersons such as successful merchants and craftspeople to enter a monastery for the months of the rainy season and then go back to their work. All Buddhists, whether they are monastic or laypersons, follow the path that leads to release from suffering. In following this path, they are said to be "taking refuge" in the Three Jewels—the Buddha, the dharma, and the sangha.

THE UNIVERSAL APPEAL OF BUDDHISM

Buddhism has a universal appeal. It recognizes the suffering that all people endure and provides a way to overcome it. Anyone can practice it, for as the Buddha said, "My doctrine makes no distinction between high and low, rich and poor; it is like the sky, it has room for all; like water it washes all alike."

In Asia, its birthplace, it has recently begun to flourish again in countries such

THE THREE JEWELS

Amid all the different forms and practices of Buddhism, one of the few things all agree on is that a Buddhist "takes refuge" in the Three Jewels. These are the Buddha, the dharma, and the sangha. Indeed, many Buddhists recite the phrase "I take refuge in the Buddha, I take refuge in the dharma, and I take refuge in the sangha" as a daily prayer. When Buddhists speak of taking refuge, they mean following the path that leads to the end of suffering—nirvana. A Tibetan proverb sums up the Three Jewels: "The Buddha is the great physician; the dharma is the remedy; the sangha is the nurse who administers the remedy."

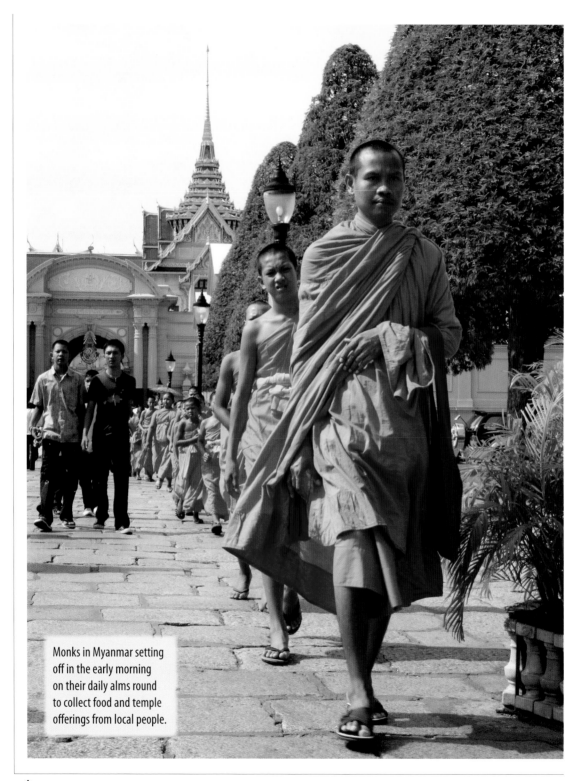

Monks in Myanmar setting off in the early morning on their daily alms round to collect food and temple offerings from local people.

as China, Mongolia, and the Russian states of Kalmyk and Buryat, where it had been almost stamped out by the communist governments.

In the West Buddhism has grown significantly since the 1960s, when it became popular among artists and writers, especially the young, for its promotion of spiritual values and promise of inner peace. In Great Britain, for example, the number of Buddhist centers has grown from about half a dozen in the 1950s to several hundred today.

The Buddha's dharma has stood the test of time. It is practical, for it provides specific action and stresses individual effort. The Buddha said that he himself could only point the way: Each person must follow the Eightfold Path on his or her own. "Look within yourself," he told his followers. "You are the Buddha."

BUDDHIST REVIVAL

Buddhism in China is now able to function relatively freely and many historic temples are being restored by the government in collaboration with the Buddhist sangha. In Mongolia the fall of communism in 1991 found Buddhism barely alive. Within a few years more than 900 temples and monasteries had been founded or reopened. Although this has now dropped down to around 600, it represents the revival by popular demand of the Mongolian faith in Buddhism.

CHAPTER 2

THE LIFE OF THE BUDDHA

Prince Siddhartha Gautama, who would become known as the Buddha, was born around the year 563 B.C.E. His birthplace was the town of Kapilavastu in what is now Nepal. Siddhartha was the son of Shuddhodana, the chief (sometimes called a raja, or king) of the Sakyas. Hence the title Sakyamuni, or "Sage of the Sakyas," by which Siddhartha was later known.

There is no doubt that Siddhartha really existed. About 250 years after his death an Indian emperor set up inscribed stone pillars at the important sites of Siddhartha's life and teachings. These are regarded as reliable historical records.

ORAL HISTORY

The details of the Buddha's life, as retold in this chapter, come from an oral tradition begun by those who actually knew and saw him. These accounts were not written down until around 500 years after his death, by which time all sorts of legends and miraculous stories had grown around him.

Stone statues of the Buddha dressed in a simple monk's robe at Ayutthaya in Thailand. Founded in 1350, Ayutthaya became the second capital of the kingdom of Siam (the former name of Thailand); the first capital of the Buddhist kingdom was at Sukhotai.

QUEEN MAYA'S DREAM

According to the Buddhist tradition Siddhartha's mother, Queen Maya, was a woman "of perfect form and bee-black tresses, fearless in heart and full of grace and virtue." One day a feeling of great peace and joy came over her. That night, while she slept, she had a wonderful dream: An elephant with six tusks, carrying a lotus flower in its trunk, touched her right side. At that moment her son was miraculously conceived.

When the queen told her husband of the dream he called Brahmins (also spelled Brahmans), or learned men, to interpret it. They predicted that the child would be either the greatest king in the world or the greatest ascetic, a holy man who practices self-denial. His name would be Siddhartha, which means "he whose aim is accomplished."

THE BIRTH OF SIDDHARTHA

Accompanied by dancing women and guards, Queen Maya went to her father's home to prepare for the birth. As she stepped from her chariot in the Lumbini Gardens she stopped to rest, taking hold of a branch of a sal tree.

Legend tells us that at that moment Buddha emerged from her right side. Without any help the infant walked seven steps in each of the four directions of the compass. In his footprints lotus flowers sprouted from the earth. The miraculous infant announced, "No further births have I to endure, for this is my last body. Now shall I destroy and pluck out by the roots the sorrow that is caused by birth and death."

Seven days after the wondrous birth Queen Maya died. Hence Mahaprajapati, Maya's sister, looked after Siddhartha.

THE GREAT RENUNCIATION

The prediction of the learned men had disturbed Siddhartha's father, King Shuddhodana. From the time of his son's birth Shuddhodana encouraged his son to follow the path of kingship. Shuddhodana surrounded his son with pleasures and granted his every wish. Never did Siddhartha see or learn about any kind of suffering or hardship. When he left the palace the king's guards went ahead of his chariot, clearing the streets of anything unpleasant or disturbing.

A Brahmin priest instructed Siddhartha in the ways of government, preparing him to govern wisely. Siddhartha also learned the arts of war—how to fight with a sword and shoot an arrow from his bow. The young man was strong and healthy, and his physical beauty and lively spirit attracted many friends. All of his companions were children of the officials of the court.

BIRTH OF A SON

When Siddhartha was about 20 he married Yasodhara, the daughter of one of the king's ministers. Their wedding feast lasted for many days, and gifts were distributed to the people of the kingdom to mark the occasion. Within a year Yasodhara bore Siddhartha's son, named Rahula, which means "fetter" or "impediment."

King Shuddhodana was pleased, for he had provided everything his son would need for happiness in his life and success as a great king. Some years passed, during which time Siddhartha lived in the palace with his wife and son, enjoying all the pleasures of a king.

OLD AGE, SICKNESS, AND DEATH

Then, when he was 29 years old, Siddhartha asked his charioteer, Channa, to take him for a ride without the consent of the king. As the prince rode through the city he saw three things that he had never seen before. One was an old man, one was a man suffering from illness, and the third was a corpse surrounded by mourners.

Siddhartha asked Channa to explain the meaning of these strange sights. Channa responded that old age, sickness, and death were natural and unavoidable things that came to all people. They were to be endured.

Shocked, Siddhartha returned to the palace and thought about what he had seen. For the first time he confronted the reality of

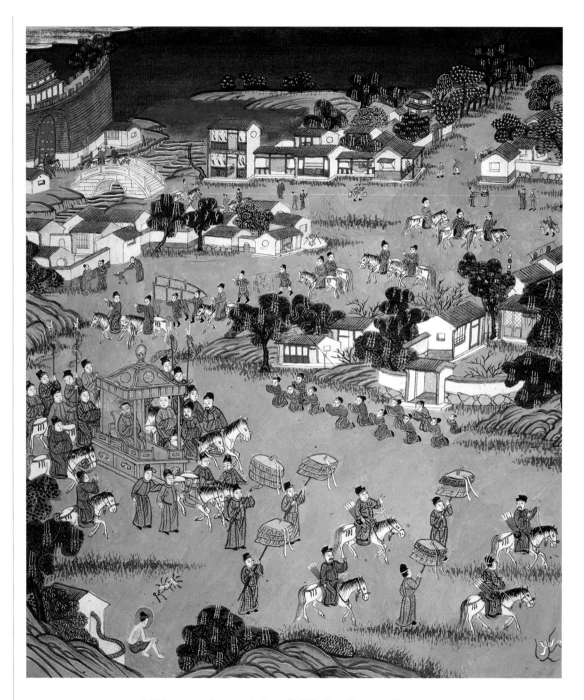

A 19th-century Chinese painting called *The Great Departure,* illustrating
Prince Siddhartha leaving his father's palace after renouncing the luxury
into which he had been born to take on the life of a wandering holy man.
Tradition holds that the circumstances of the event were far more austere.

life: "Everything is transient; nothing is permanent in this world . . . Knowing that, I can find delight in nothing . . . How can a man, who knows that death is quite inevitable, still feel greed in his heart, enjoy the world of senses and not weep in this great danger?"

RENOUNCING A LIFE OF PLEASURE

Once more Siddhartha asked Channa to take him into the city. This time he saw the last of the "Four Sights" that changed his life. This was a wandering holy man, an ascetic, with no possessions. The man had shaved his head, wore only a ragged yellow robe, and carried a walking staff. Siddhartha stopped his chariot and questioned the man. The ascetic told the prince, "I am . . . terrified by birth and death and therefore have adopted a homeless life to win salvation . . . I search for the most blessed state in which suffering, old age, and death are unknown."

That very night Siddhartha resolved to renounce the life of pleasure in the palace. He silently kissed his sleeping wife Yasodhara and his young son and ordered Channa to drive him out of the city. Legend claims that celestial beings held up the hooves of the horses so that their clatter would not wake the guards. At the edge of a forest Siddhartha took off his jeweled sword, cut off his hair and beard, and discarded his princely garments. He put on the yellow robe of a holy man and told Channa to take his possessions back to his father.

KARMA

When a soul is reborn it may enter a body in a higher or lower state of existence than its previous one. The new body may be that of a king, a beggar, or even an animal or insect. The determining factor of a soul's new existence is the quality of life led by the individual soul in its previous existence. This is called the law of karma. Simply put, karma consists of the individual's thoughts, words, and deeds in his or her previous existences. If the karma has been good, the soul will be reborn in a higher form. Conversely, if the karma has been bad, the soul is punished (pays a "karmic price") by being reborn in a lower form.

THE GREAT RETIREMENT

Siddhartha wandered through northeastern India seeking out holy men, who taught him ancient Indian techniques of meditation. However his main quest was to find the answer to the problem of suffering. He wanted to know why people suffered and how this suffering could end.

Siddhartha studied the ancient teachings of India. He was most influenced by the concept of samsara. Samsara is a belief that after death a person's innermost essence, or soul, transmigrates into a new body—it is born again. Another name for this process is reincarnation. Every action, thought, and deed has an effect in this life and the next life. This is the law of karma. If the quality of one life has been good it will lead to a better rebirth.

FOUR CASTES

The law of karma also had social implications. Indian society was strictly divided into four castes, or classes. At the top were the Brahmins—priests and religious teachers. The second caste included the warriors and rulers. It was within this caste that Siddhartha was born. The third and fourth castes were the merchants and workers (laborers, craftsmen, farmers, and so on). At the very bottom were people who were literally outcastes, below the four castes, whose station in life made them impure.

In a single lifetime it was impossible to rise within the caste system. By law and tradition the members of each caste were strictly separated from the others. People of different castes did not marry, eat together, or have physical contact with one another. If a person violated the caste rules he or she had to undergo rituals of purification. The only way to move up was to accumulate good karma and be reborn into a higher caste.

MOKSHA—RELEASE

Some believed that samsara—this process of life, death, and rebirth—was an endless chain of existence. It would continue forever, from life to life. Around the time of Siddhartha's life, however, new teachings—later set down in scriptures called the Upanishads—were being developed. The Upanishadic teachers developed the idea of *moksha,* or release. By leading a highly spiritual life (or several lives) a soul could be reunited with Brahman, the Ultimate Reality. The cycle of samsara would be broken.

SIDDHARTHA'S SELF-DENIAL

Attracted by this idea, Siddhartha adopted a life of extreme self-denial and penances, meditating constantly. He settled on the bank of the Nairanjana River, determined to force himself into

A depiction of Siddhartha when his body wasted away during the six years he spent fasting, before he realized that the path to wisdom did not lie in extremes.

the state of mind that would lead to *moksha*. For six years, through rain and wind, hot and cold weather, he stayed there, eating and drinking only enough to stay alive. His body became emaciated and his former physical strength left him. His holiness was so evident that five other holy men joined him, hoping to learn from his example.

THE ENLIGHTENMENT

One day, the Buddhist tradition holds, Siddhartha realized that his years of penance had only weakened his body. In such a state of physical exhaustion he could not meditate properly. He stood up and stepped into the river to bathe. However he was so weak that he could not raise himself out of the water. The Buddhist

A pilgrim meditating at Bodhgaya in northern India. In the shrine at Bodhgaya is a tree believed to grow on the site of the original Bodhi tree under which Buddha gained enlightenment.

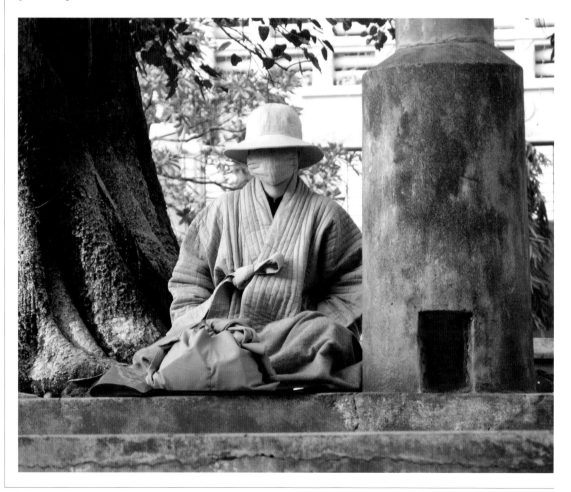

scriptures say that the trees on the riverbank bent their branches down so that he could reach them.

At that moment a milkmaid named Nandabala came into sight. She offered Siddhartha a bowl of milk and rice and he accepted it gratefully. When the five holy men who had been his pupils saw this they left, because they thought he had abandoned his quest to achieve true holiness, or *moksha*.

Refreshed by the meal, Siddhartha sat down under a bo, or fig, tree (known to Buddhists as the Bodhi tree, the tree of enlightenment) and resolved that he would not arise until he had found the answer he had sought for so long.

The Buddhist scriptures say that Mara, an evil god who constantly tempted people with desire, saw that Siddhartha was near his goal. Mara sent his three sons and three daughters to tempt Siddhartha. They tormented him with thirst, lust, and discontent, offering all sorts of pleasures to distract him and stop him achieving his aims.

However Siddhartha was not swayed by them. He entered a state of deep meditation, in which he recalled all his previous rebirths. He gained knowledge of the cycle of births and deaths and the certainty that he had cast off the ignorance and passion of the "I" self that bound him to the world. At last he had attained enlightenment.

As tradition has it, the Buddha could then have cast off his body and his existence. Instead, however, he made a great act of self-sacrifice. Having discovered the way to end his own suffering, he turned back, determined to share his enlightenment with others so that all living souls could end the cycles of their own rebirth and suffering. He thus set an example of compassion and wisdom or self-knowledge for others that would be a hallmark of his followers.

THE ENLIGHTENED ONE

The Buddha's enlightenment under the Bodhi tree was the beginning of the history of Buddhism as a religion. Siddhartha became the Buddha, the "enlightened one." His own desire and suffering were over and, as the Buddha, he attained nirvana. In the Buddha's words, "There is a sphere which is neither earth, nor water, nor fire, nor air . . . which is neither this world nor the other world, neither sun nor moon. I deny that it is coming or going, enduring death or birth. It is only the end of suffering."

A Buddhist *tanka* painted by Tibetan monks. A *tanka* illustrates stories about the Buddha and events in his life, some of which can be seen in the arc around the head of the Buddha. *Tankas* are also used as a focus for meditation.

SETTING IN MOTION THE WHEEL OF DOCTRINE

Buddha went to the city of Sarnath, where he found the five ascetics who had deserted him earlier. They were sitting in a deer park. Seeing him approach, they decided not to greet him by the respectful title they had used to address him before. However when he appeared before them, they saw signs on his body and head that indicated he had risen to a higher state of holiness.

The Buddha began to teach them what he had discovered. He took a handful of rice grains and drew a wheel on the ground. This represented the wheel of life that went on for existence after existence. (The symbol of the wheel is often used to stand for Buddhist teaching.) This preaching was called his Deer Park Sermon, or "Setting in Motion the Wheel of Doctrine."

THE MIDDLE WAY

Siddhartha Gautama revealed that he had become the Buddha. He described the life of pleasure that he had first known and then the life of severe asceticism that he had practiced. Neither of these was the true path to nirvana. Instead the Buddha advised the Middle Way, which avoids both extremes. "To satisfy the necessities of life is not evil," the Buddha said. "To keep the body in good health is a duty, for otherwise we shall not be able to trim the lamp of wisdom, and keep our mind strong and clear."

THE FOUR NOBLE TRUTHS

The Four Noble Truths are:

1. Suffering consists of disease, old age, and death; of separation from those we love; of craving what we cannot obtain; and of hating what we cannot avoid.
2. All suffering is caused by desire and the attempt to satisfy our desires.
3. Therefore, suffering can be overcome by ceasing to desire.
4. The way to end desire is to follow the Eightfold Path.

THE EIGHTFOLD PATH

The Eightfold Path is a series of eight stages that lead to the end of desire. Of these the first stages are attainable in everyday life; the later ones require more effort and concentration. Like many of Buddha's teachings they appear simple at first but take on subtle and intricate meaning when studied closely.

The Eightfold Path is:
1. Right opinion
2. Right intentions
3. Right speech
4. Right conduct
5. Right livelihood
6. Right effort
7. Right mindfulness
8. Right concentration

The Buddha explained the Four Noble Truths and the Eightfold Path that were the heart of his teaching. The Four Noble Truths were the Buddha's analysis of the cause of suffering. The Eightfold Path was the solution. Together they formed the dharma, or the doctrine of Buddhism.

STAGES OF THE EIGHTFOLD PATH

The first stage, right opinion, concerns understanding the Four Truths. Then, through right intentions, a person decides to set his or her life on the correct path. Right speech consists of not lying, not criticizing others unjustly, and not using harsh language or gossiping. Right conduct means abstaining from killing, stealing, cruelty, or lustful activities. To follow right livelihood a person must earn a living in a way that does not harm any living thing. To practice right effort a person must conquer all evil thoughts and strive to arouse and maintain only good thoughts. Right mindfulness has a special meaning in Buddhism, in which a person becomes intensely aware of all the states of his or her body, feeling, and mind. That leads to the final stage, right concentration, which is deep meditation that leads to a higher stage of consciousness. A person who practices right concentration will come to the enlightenment that Siddhartha attained.

BUDDHA'S TRAVELS AND TEACHINGS

The five ascetics immediately recognized that the Buddha had found the correct way. They became his first disciples. For the next 45 years he traveled through northeastern India, preaching the dharma and answering the questions of those who wished to learn it.

In his teachings the Buddha retained many elements of the religious teachings of India of his time, including the concepts of samsara and karma. However, the Buddhist dharma differed from them in certain important respects. The Buddha challenged the authority of the Brahmins,

Health

Health is the greatest possession.
Contentment is the greatest treasure.
Confidence is the greatest friend.
Nirvana is the greatest joy.

—From the *Dhammapada* (15:204)

the highest caste in Indian society. He opposed the animal sacrifices to the various gods, which only Brahmin priests could perform. In contrast the Buddha told his followers not to kill any living creature. In addition the Buddha did not accept the Brahmins' special role as interpreters of religious truth. Instead the Buddha stressed that anyone, regardless of caste, who followed the Eightfold Path could achieve nirvana.

SKANDHAS

The Buddha also questioned the idea of the atman, or soul—the individual consciousness that was reborn again and again. He denied that there was any personal, eternal soul or permanent self. Instead the Buddha compared the individual to a cart. A cart was made up of different elements—wheels, body, yoke. Separately they were not a cart. Only when they were together did they form a cart. In the same way, Buddha taught, an individual is composed of five elements called *skandhas,* which were constantly in a state of change. The *skandhas* were form and matter, sensations, ideas, emotions, and consciousness. What was reborn over and over were groups of ever-changing *skandhas,* influenced by karma. Thus, the *skandhas* reborn were not exactly the same as the *skandhas* that had died.

The Buddha declared that by following his Eightfold Path people would lose their false idea of self and achieve nirvana. When a person reached nirvana the "cart" would dissolve. After that a person would no longer accumulate bad karma, even if his life continued.

PARABLES AND STORIES

As for the concept of Brahman itself, which we might liken to a supreme being, the Buddha refused to consider whether such a universal soul existed. Once, when a religious scholar pressed the Buddha to debate the existence of Brahman, he replied that the scholar was like a man who finds himself in a burning house. The scholar wanted to find out who set the fire or how it started, when he should be thinking first of getting out of the house. The Hindu

Parable of the Mustard Seed

Once a distraught woman brought the body of her dead son to the Buddha. She begged him to bring the boy back to life. The Buddha asked the woman to bring him a tiny mustard seed. However he made one condition: the seed must be one that came from a house in which no death had ever occurred. The woman searched but could not find such a house. Instead she saw people who had suffered losses like her own. In her search her own pain lessened as compassion for the pain of others increased. The Buddha wanted her to realize that death was normal and universal. Only through facing the human situation "as it really is" could she start her own journey on the Eightfold Path.

goal of *moksha*—or union of the soul with Brahman—was replaced in Buddhism by the goal of achieving nirvana.

The simplicity of the Buddha's teaching, its emphasis on personal action, and the Buddha's opposition to the caste system soon won him many followers. Like other religious teachers, Buddha often used stories or parables to explain his doctrine. In the Parable of the Mustard Seed the Buddha taught the lesson of facing and accepting suffering.

BHIKKHUS

Beginning with the five disciples he spoke to in the Deer Park, certain people embraced the Buddha's teachings so completely that they accompanied him everywhere. He set rules of conduct for them, thus organizing the sangha, which became a community of monks (later nuns as well). The members of the sangha are known as *bhikkhus*. The sangha served two functions. First, the monks were charged with preserving and teaching the dharma. Second, the sangha enabled *bhikkhus* to concentrate on the goal of nirvana. Only people who spent time in meditation could achieve the last two steps of the Eightfold Path.

The Buddha made another break with tradition when he was persuaded by his closest disciple Ananda to permitted women to join the sangha. The first Buddhist nun was the Buddha's aunt, who had raised him.

THE FIVE PRECEPTS

The Buddha recognized that not everyone could give up his or her everyday life to become part of the sangha. He also accepted the laity—followers (*upasaka*) who believed his teachings but did not follow the strict rule of the sangha. People in everyday life could achieve merit by practicing good works and building good karma. In a future rebirth they would be able to dedicate themselves as monks or nuns to seek nirvana. The Buddha encouraged the laity to follow as perfect a life as they could. As a guide to everyday behavior the Buddha prescribed Five Precepts, or rules:

1. To refrain from taking life.
2. To refrain from taking what is not given.
3. To refrain from sexual misconduct.
4. To refrain from false speech.
5. To refrain from intoxicating things that cloud the mind.

THE *PARINIRVANA*

During the Buddha's travels he returned to his birthplace in Kapilavastu. His father, Shuddhodana, was mortified to see his son begging for food. "No one in our family," said the king, "has ever lived by begging." However the Buddha kissed his father's foot and said, "You belong to a noble line of kings. But I belong to the lineage of Buddhas, and thousands of those have lived on alms."

Shuddhodana remembered and acted upon the prophecy at Siddhartha's conception and became reconciled with his son. The Buddha's wife Yasodhara and son Rahula both joined the sangha, as did his cousin Ananda, who became the Buddha's most faithful attendant during the later years of his life.

THE END OF THE JOURNEY

When the Buddha was about 80 a blacksmith named Cuanda gave him a meal that caused him to become ill. The Buddha forced himself to walk on to the village of Kushinagara, where at last he lay down to rest in a grove of shala trees. As a crowd of

SIMPLE POSSESSIONS

Early Buddhist monks and nuns followed the Buddha's example of wandering from place to place spreading his teaching. They were allowed to possess only an alm's bowl, a razor, a needle, a strainer, a staff, a toothpick, and a robe. (The strainer was to remove insects that fell into their drinks, so they would not be consumed and killed.)

During India's long, hot rainy season, the members of the sangha settled in *viharas,* or resting places. These were the beginnings of the great monasteries that are today found in many parts of Asia.

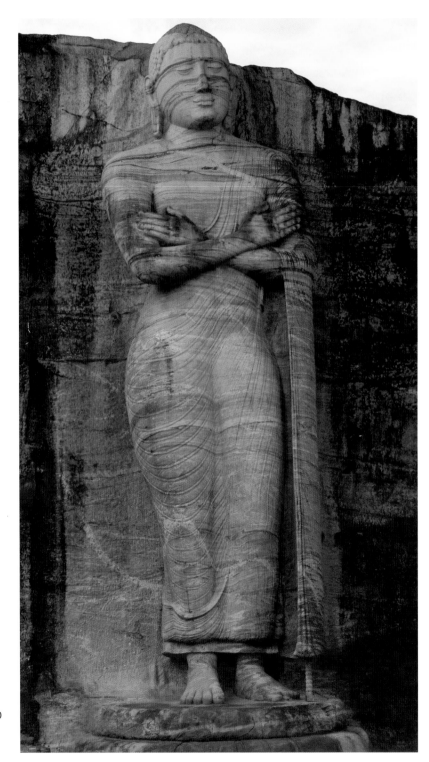

A 23-foot-high granite statue of Ananda, Buddha's cousin and one of his major disciples, at Polonnaruwa in Sri Lanka. This statue is one of a series of four carved into the natural rock in the 12th century.

followers gathered around him, he lay on his right side. Though it was not the season for blooming, the trees sprouted blossoms and showered them upon him. The scene has often been the inspiration for Buddhist artists.

BUDDHA'S FINAL WORDS

Buddha told Ananda, "I am old and my journey is near its end. My body is like a worn-out cart held together only by the help of leather straps." Three times he asked the people gathered around him if they had any more questions about his teaching. Everyone remained silent.

The Buddha spoke his final words: "Everything that has been created is subject to decay and death. Everything is transitory. Work out your own salvation with diligence."

After passing through several states of meditation the Buddha died—or, as Buddhists say, he reached his *parinirvana,* "the cessation of perception and sensation."

During his long lifetime the Buddha never traveled farther than 250 miles from Sarnath, the city where his teaching ministry began. However, he had set in motion a religious movement that would spread throughout the world and still remains a vital force 2,500 years after his death.

CHAPTER 3

THE SPREAD OF BUDDHISM

The Buddha urged his followers, "Go forth for the gain of the many, for the welfare of many, in compassion for the world. Preach the glorious doctrine; proclaim the life of holiness." By the time of his death more than 500 monks lived in monasteries in the area where the Buddha had preached. Today this region forms the Indian state of Bihar, whose name comes from *vihara,* meaning "Buddhist monastery." From here Buddhism began to spread westward through northern India.

About 200 years after the death of the Buddha political developments encouraged the spread of the dharma. Chandragupta Maurya conquered much of northern India and created a strong, centralized empire. When Chandragupta's grandson Asoka became emperor around 270 B.C.E., the stage was set for Buddhism to move beyond the boundaries of India. The story of King Asoka's conversion is central to the historical progress of Buddhism.

Portrait of a Burmese novice monk in traditional robes. In Buddhist countries young boys often join a monastery for several months or several years. In countries such as Thailand and Myanmar (formerly Burma) boys usually spend time in monasteries during the three months of the rainy season.

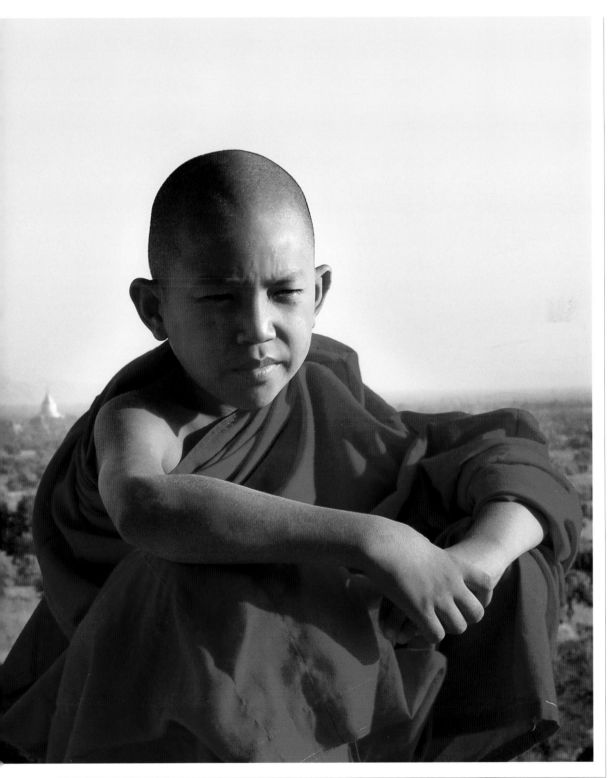

Asoka was an ambitious man. Through conquest he expanded the Mauryan Empire, absorbing central India as well as parts of many of the countries on modern India's northern border. He waged his fiercest campaign against the Kalingas, who lived in today's Orissa, in east central India. The struggle was so bloody that more than 100,000 Kalingas were slaughtered.

His experience of walking across the battlefield and seeing the carnage brought about a spiritual transformation in Asoka. He became a follower of Buddhism and set up a stone pillar expressing remorse for his deeds: "After the conquest of Kalinga, the Beloved of the Gods (Asoka) began to follow Righteousness (dharma), to love Righteousness, and to give instruction in Righteousness. Now the Beloved of the Gods regrets the conquest of Kalinga, for when an independent country is conquered people are killed, they die or are deported, and that the Beloved of the Gods finds very painful and grievous."

A MODEL BUDDHIST RULER

Asoka's conversion was no empty gesture, and thereafter he carried out policies designed to benefit his subjects. Along the roads throughout his empire he ordered shelters built for travelers and banyan trees planted to provide shade for the footsore and weary. Asoka banned animal sacrifices and became a vegetarian himself. He abolished many cruel punishments for criminals. Hospitals were founded to serve both animals and humans. His government undertook the financial support of Buddhist monasteries. Asoka's actions made him the model Buddhist ruler. Later Buddhist kings throughout Asia would emulate his example.

As a permanent record of his reign Asoka erected pillars throughout his

ASOKA'S EDICTS

On a pillar that still stands in Delhi, King Asoka ordered his philosophy inscribed in stone: "In religion is the chief excellence. Religion consists in good works, mercy, charity, purity, and chastity. It consists in benevolence to the poor and to the afflicted, kindness to animals, to birds and to all creatures. Let all pay attention to this edict and let it endure for ages to come. He who acts in conformity with it shall attain to eternal happiness." This indeed is a noble statement of the ethics of Buddhism.

empire. Inscribed in the language of its people, a form of the Pali language, they proclaimed his achievements and ideals. Among these ideals was tolerance of all religions.

BUDDHIST MISSIONARIES

Wishing to carry the wisdom of the Buddha to the world, Asoka sent out missionaries in all directions. This historical event began the spread of the religion beyond its homeland. Some of

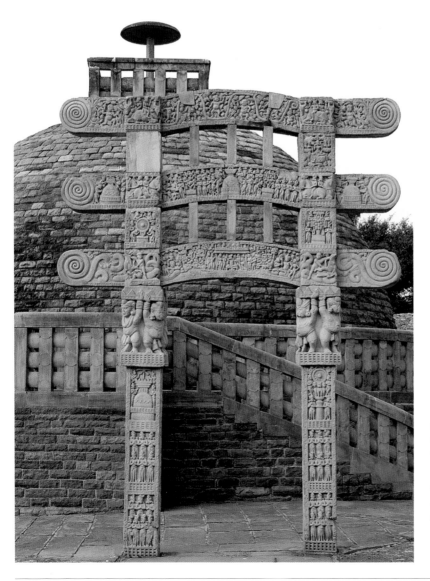

Exquisitely carved with Buddhist symbols and Jataka stories (which describe the previous lives of the Buddha), this 18-foot- (5.5-meter-) high gateway to the largest dome stupa in the world is in Sanchi, India. The stupa is believed to have been originally constructed at the request of King Asoka.

Asoka's missionaries went as far west as Syria, Egypt, and the Greek world; others traveled south and north. Asoka began the process of making Buddhism a religion that would have followers throughout Asia.

Buddhism spread along two major routes—one to the north across the landmass of Asia and the other to the south across land and sea to southeastern Asia.

SRI LANKA

By tradition Asoka's son Mahinda was a *bhikkhu,* or monk. His father entrusted him with carrying the dharma to Ceylon. Known today as Sri Lanka, Ceylon is a beautiful island off the tip of southern India. When Mahinda arrived he was courteously received by the king, Tissa, at his capital at Anuradhapura. The king was impressed by the Buddhist teachings and converted in 247 B.C.E. Enthusiastic crowds gathered to hear Mahinda preach the dharma. Soothsayers predicted, "These *bhikkhus* will be lords upon this island."

CREATING BUDDHIST ROOTS

King Tissa invited other Buddhist missionaries and donated a park for a *vihara*. This monastery, the Mahavihara, became the center of Buddhism on the island. In his enthusiasm King Tissa asked Mahinda whether the devotion shown by his people meant that Buddhism had struck deep roots in his country. Mahinda answered, "Not yet, Your Majesty. It has certainly sprung roots but they have not yet grown deep into the soil. Only when a *sima* (a monastery with the authority to ordain new monks) has been established and when a son born in Sri Lanka of Sri Lankan parents becomes a monk in Sri Lanka, only then will it be true to say that the roots of the dharma are deeply embedded here." Within a short time these conditions were met.

BODHI TREE AND PRECIOUS RELICS

Mahinda's sister, Sanghamitta, a Buddhist nun, soon followed her brother to Sri Lanka. Buddhist tradition says that before she left

India she picked a slip of the sacred Bodhi tree under which Siddhartha Gautama had reached enlightenment. This was planted at a monastery in Anuradhapura. Today an enormous tree on this site is claimed to be the same one. Later saplings from this tree were planted throughout the island, providing a linkage through nature with the origins of Buddhism. Over time Sri Lanka received other precious relics of the Buddha. These included the Buddha's begging bowl, his tooth, and a collarbone.

From the beginning Buddhism was incorporated as the state religion of Sri Lanka. The Sri Lankan kings and nobles practiced Buddhism and were patrons of Buddhist culture. Buddhism's close relationship with the ruling class has given it a longer continuous existence there than in any other country in the world. Because the religion virtually died out within India, Sri Lanka's sangha takes pride in preserving the early form of the monastic Buddhist discipline.

SOUTHEAST ASIA

The region known as Southeast Asia stretches from Myanmar (formerly Burma) to Indonesia. Historically it has been influenced to a great degree by India—so much so that it is often called "Greater India." Indian merchants and monks brought not only religion but also their civilization—writing, arts, and methods of ruling. Buddhism and Hinduism often coexisted in the same areas, along with the preexisting belief in animism, the belief that spirits inhabit all things.

BURMA

Buddhism came to the country known today as Myanmar before the Burmese people did. When Asoka's missionaries arrived the land was inhabited by the Mon people. By the ninth century, when ethnic Burmese moved into the land from the mountains to the north, the Mons were practicing both Hinduism and Buddhism.

The Burmese gradually established their own kingdom. A great Burmese ruler, King Anawrahta (r. 1044–77), was converted to Buddhism in 1056 by a monk from the neighboring Mon kingdom of Thaton. Anawrahta sent an envoy to Thaton to ask for scriptures of the religion but was turned down. In a very un-Buddhist manner, Anawrahta invaded Thaton and carried its king and library back to his capital at Pagan. Anawrahta's conversion was a turning point for Buddhism in Burma, beginning a religious tradition that has remained strong to this day. The Burmese people have a proverb: "To be Burmese is to be Buddhist."

Monks and pilgrims at Shwedagon Pagoda built on Singuttara Hill in Rangoon (now Yangon), Myanmar. The pagoda, built of brick and covered entirely in gold, houses precious Buddhist relics and is believed to date back more than 2,000 years.

THAILAND

In the 11th century the Thai people migrated from southern China into today's Thailand. At that time the region was under the authority of the Khmer king. A Thai ruler, Rama Khamheng (ca. 1275–1317), freed the country from the Khmer power. Khamheng became an ardent Buddhist and made Buddhism the state religion. Khamheng's grandson invited monks from Sri Lanka, by then famous for their learning, to come to Thailand to strengthen the purity of the Thai sangha. From that time on Thailand has been a staunchly Buddhist country whose kings have linked their power to the religion.

CAMBODIA

The Khmer people of Cambodia were also influenced by Indian civilization. From the beginning of the sixth century Khmer kings ruled a large area from their capital at Angkor. They devoted much of their wealth to the construction of magnificent buildings, the most famous of which is the temple called Angkor Wat, which was used by both Hindus and Buddhists. Hinduism remained the stronger of the two religions until King Jayavarman Paramesvara came to the throne in 1327. He embraced Buddhism, and the Cambodians have followed his example ever since.

LAOS AND INDONESIA

King Jayavarman had his daughter marry a king named Fa Ngum, who had merged several small states into the country of Laos. Jayavarman urged Fa Ngum to protect Buddhism and to rule his kingdom according to the religion's principles. He sent his son-in-law a statue of the Buddha that came from Sri Lanka. Called the Luang Prabang, the statue was set up in Fa Ngum's capital, which was renamed in its honor. Buddhism has remained the predominant religion of Laos.

Many large seafaring empires were established in the islands that today make up the nation of Indonesia. Here too Hinduism and Buddhism coexisted; but in the eighth century Buddhism was adopted by the Sailendra ruling dynasty of the island of Java.

Under the Sailendra's sponsorship, mammoth Buddhist temple-monastery complexes were built. Among them—still standing today—is the largest Buddhist monument in the world, Borobodur. At the end of the 13th century Islam arrived on the island. Over time it became the predominant religion, although a few Buddhists remain.

ALONG THE SILK ROAD

Northwest of the Indian heartland lies an area that was sometimes called Gandhara, or Bactria. Today it includes northwest India, northern Pakistan, Afghanistan, and parts of Central Asia. In ancient times this region was a major crossroads between East and West. Here the cultures of India, Persia, and the Greco-Roman West all mingled. Alexander the Great invaded and conquered the region in 326 B.C.E. When Alexander left, some of his generals remained as governors. The region included the western section of the Silk Road, the ancient trail that led through fearsome deserts and mountains to serve as the land link between China and the West.

THE BACTRIAN EMPIRE

After Asoka's death the Mauryan Empire declined. In the chaos of that time the kingdom of Bactria arose between the Oxus River and the Hindu Kush Mountains. Bactria was ruled by Greek descendants of Alexander the Great's soldiers.

King Milinda (also known as King Menander), who ruled Bactria about 155 B.C.E., was afflicted with a sense of spiritual sickness. He searched vainly for some kind of cure. A Buddhist monk named Nagasena arrived in the kingdom and brought the remedy. Nagasena explained Buddhist dharma to Milinda and gained a convert. The record of Nagasena's arguments, called Conversations with Milinda, became part of the Buddhist sacred writings.

Milinda became an ardent patron of Buddhism. His coinage in later years holds a picture of a wheel, a Buddhist symbol for dharma. As an old man he reputedly handed over his kingdom to his son and became a member of the sangha.

Invaders overran the Bactrian Empire and control of the territory changed hands many times. Around the middle of the first century of the common era, fierce warriors related to the Huns established the Kushan Empire. The Kushans controlled a far larger territory than Milinda had. King Kanishka, who ruled in the first and second centuries, was a fierce warrior. Ruling from his capital Purushapura (today's Peshawar), Kanishka extended his kingdom east to Kathgar, Yarkand, and Khotan—all oases on

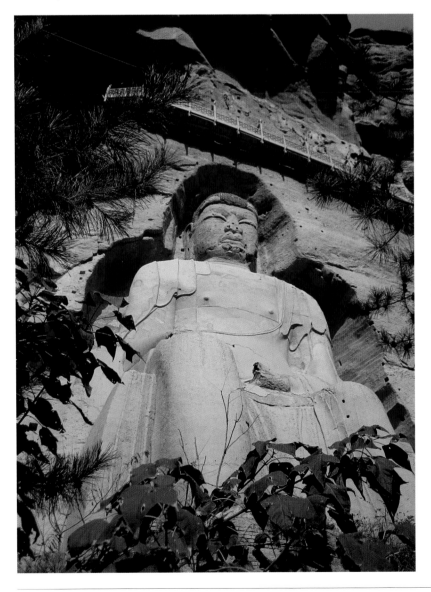

Standing more than 75 feet (23 meters) high, this seated Buddha is carved into the side of a mountain at Bingling Si Temple near Lanzhou, Gansu Province in China. Lanzhou lay along the Silk Road, whose name derives from the importance of Chinese silk as merchandise carried by the camel caravans passed along it. Ideas as well as goods were exchanged along the road. The Silk Road became the major route for the northern spread of Buddhism.

the Silk Road. Much like Asoka, however, the king experienced a religious crisis and converted to Buddhism.

Kanishka became a great patron of the religion. He had sacred Buddhist writings inscribed on copper plates and displayed in his capital. (Today they survive only in Chinese translations.) From monasteries established during his reign (such as Bamiyan in today's Afghanistan), monks fanned out through Central Asia. They converted kings and regional leaders, translated scriptures into the native languages, and brought the art of writing to the area. The oases of Central Asia became centers of Buddhism, and the arts flourished. In the eighth century, however, Muslim warriors conquered Central Asia. Over time Buddhism was supplanted by Islam. However by then Buddhist *bhikkhus* had already gone farther east on the Silk Road, spreading their religion to China and other lands.

CHINA

In the first century of the common era, according to Chinese legend Mingdi, a Han emperor of China, had a dream: A huge figure, radiant as the sun, appeared to the emperor. The next day he ordered agents to go west to find the source of his vision. After much wandering on the Silk Road the agents came upon two *bhikkhus* with a white horse, a picture of the Buddha, and holy Buddhist writings. The *bhikkhus* agreed to return with the agents to Luoyang, China's capital. There the emperor recognized the figure of the Buddha from his dream. He asked the monks to translate their scriptures into Chinese, and they set to work in a building that became known as the White Horse Temple. (Today there is still a White Horse Temple on that site.)

A THIRD TRUTH

During the Han dynasty (202 B.C.E.–220 C.E.) China was one of the great civilizations of the world. It had already developed two philosophies that guided its culture. Both had been founded by men who lived at approximately the same time as the Buddha— Confucius and Laozi. Confucius, the founder of Confucianism, described the proper relationships between people, which if followed would bring harmony to society and government. Laozi, on the other hand, believed that harmony was best gained by following the way (the Dao) of nature. Daoism and Confucianism were equally respected by the Chinese, who had no difficulty in accepting separate truths that answered different needs for different areas of life. Buddhism neither contradicted nor replaced either of these philosophies. In time it was accepted by the Chinese as one of the "Three Great Truths."

CHINESE PILGRIMS TO INDIA

After the Han dynasty was overthrown China was disunited for the next 350 years. During this time of conflict and turmoil Buddhism's message sank deep roots among the Chinese people. Sanghas were formed and Indian missionaries came to teach. Translation bureaus were set up to render the Buddhist religious texts into Chinese.

In the early-5th century C.E. a Chinese monk called Faxian made the hazardous journey from China to India to bring back Buddhist texts. About 250 years later Xuanzang, whom the Chinese call "the prince of pilgrims," made his famous journey to India. Xuanzang entered India through the old kingdom of Bactria. He visited the place in which Kanishka, then still fierce and unconverted, had held a Chinese hostage. Treating his captive with special respect, Kanishka had erected a building to hold him. This dwelling was now a monastery called Serika, which was the Bactrians' word for China. The face of the Chinese prisoner could still be seen painted on the wall. Xuanzang, as the first Chinese visitor to the monastery, was greeted warmly by the monks, who explained its history.

FAXIAN'S JOURNEY

Chinese monks themselves made the trek to India to bring back precious Buddhist texts. The journey was hazardous; the monks had to cross deserts and high mountains to reach their destination. Faxian, who traveled for 15 years (399–414) on his mission, described the terrors of the Gobi Desert: "There are a great many evil spirits and also hot winds; those who encounter them perish to a man. There are neither birds above nor beasts below. Gazing on all sides as far as the eye can reach in order to mark the track, no guidance is to be obtained save from the rotting bones of dead men, which point the way."

XUANZANG REACHES THE GANGES

While Xuanzang was traveling on the Ganges River he was captured by pirates who were looking for a victim to sacrifice to a local deity. As they began to make their sacrificial fire Xuanzang went into deep meditation and a miracle occurred. Suddenly a cyclone blew up and smashed the pirate ship on the shore. The pirates were so terrified that they released Xuanzang.

When Xuanzang arrived at the Bodhi tree where Siddhartha had achieved enlightenment, he was overcome by emotion. He wept as he thought of his own failings. If he had not been sinful in a previous existence he might have lived in the perfect days when the Buddha was alive. "I wonder," he thought, "in what troubled whirl of birth and death I was caught when Buddha achieved enlightenment."

RETURN TO CHINA

Xuanzang returned to China in 645 and received a hero's welcome in Chang'an, the capital of the Tang dynasty. He brought back an enormous number of manuscripts and spent the rest of

Ruins in Xinjiang Province in southwest China. Xinjiang lay along the Silk Road, the name given to the trade routes that linked China with India and western Asia and Europe.

his life translating and teaching. He hastened the development of Chinese branches of Buddhism and became a genuine folk hero himself. His adventures on his journey became celebrated in art and folklore. The great Chinese novel *Monkey* describes his pilgrimage in allegorical fashion. The novel's mixture of earthy humor and religious philosophy exemplifies the down-to-earth quality of Chinese Buddhism. In addition the writings of Xuanzang himself provide a vivid picture of Buddhism in Central Asia and India in the seventh century.

THE TANG DYNASTY

The Tang dynasty (618–927) was a period of Chinese cultural splendor and a high point of Buddhist influence. Buddhism was then at the center of Chinese religious and intellectual life. Most emperors—including the only female "Son of Heaven," Empress Wu—were patrons of the religion. Some rulers maintained "state temples," where Buddhist rituals were performed for the well-being of the country. The monasteries became the most important social-service agencies of their time. The sangha maintained hospitals, provided aid for the poor, and distributed food in times of famine. In the year 729 a census counted 126,100 monks and nuns.

NEW SCHOOLS OF BUDDHISM

The Chinese Buddhists were now ready to go beyond translating Indian texts. They began to write interpretations of the dharma and to develop new schools of Buddhism. The invention of printing increased the availability of texts and helped to spread the religion further. The very first printed books were collections of Buddhist scriptures.

Nalanda University

Xuanzang visited Nalanda, the great Buddhist university where scholars from many Buddhist lands came to study. He stayed there for five years, studying and debating the finer points of doctrine with other scholars. Xuanzang's description of Nalanda is the best source we have for this great Buddhist center:

"From morning to night (the bhikkhus) engage in discussion; the old and the younger mutually help one another. Learned men from different cities, who desire to acquire renown . . . come here and then their wisdom spreads far and wide. For this reason they style themselves Nalanda students, and are honored as a consequence."

In the waning years of the Tang dynasty, however, Buddhism came under attack. Some Confucian scholars criticized it as a foreign import, polluting the true Chinese ways. The Buddhist monasteries, which had grown in wealth and power, excited envy. Because so many men and women had chosen the life of the sangha, Buddhism was accused of weakening the Confucian ideal of family and the obligation to produce sons. In 845 the emperor ordered the monasteries closed and all monks and nuns to return to regular life. Although Buddhism survived it went into a decline over the next thousand years. It would never again play as central a role in Chinese life. However, Chinese ideas continued to enrich newer interpretations of Buddhist thought.

The Chinese version of Buddhism, which came from India before 100 C.E. and was influenced by Confucianism and Daoism, became important in East Asia during the 300s. It was this version that eventually spread to Korea, Japan, and Vietnam.

The Mogao Caves at Dunhuang in Gansu Province, China. The oasis town of Dunhuang was an important stopping point for caravans traveling along the Silk Road. From the fourth century C.E. Buddhist monks began building a monastic center by carving caves into the mountainsides, adorning them with devotional statues and paintings. This continued over the next 600 years, creating a rich and extensive collection of Buddhist art.

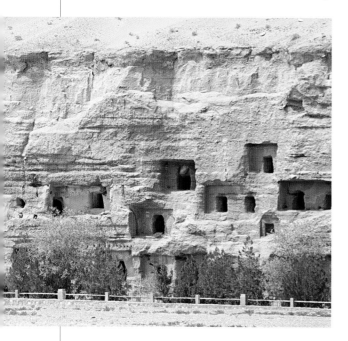

VIETNAM

Chinese missionaries brought Buddhism to the region of today's northern Vietnam, which was then a part of the Chinese Empire. (For this reason the Vietnamese form of Buddhism more closely resembles that of China, rather than that of its neighbors, Laos and Cambodia.) Like the Chinese, the Vietnamese blended Buddhism with their native religious practices. Each large village had an image of the Buddha, and members of the sangha were deeply involved in village affairs. The monks, with their knowledge of medicine and philosophy, were highly respected by the people and soon attracted followers among the aristocracy. The Buddhist monks gained popular support by sharing the Vietnamese struggle against Chinese domination and, much later, against French colonial rule.

KOREA

The peninsula of Korea was frequently under the sway of the Chinese Empire as well. By tradition a Chinese monk named Shundao (Sundo in Korean) brought Buddhism to Korea in 372. At that time there were three Korean kingdoms, and the northern two rapidly accepted the religion. The southernmost, Silla, resisted, and the people there killed a missionary from the north. However this missionary, Yi Chadon, predicted that his blood would run as white as milk to demonstrate the truth of the Buddhist dharma. When this prophecy came true the Sillans also accepted the religion. Korean Buddhism experienced a golden age from the sixth to the 14th centuries, a time when its kings were patrons of the religion.

JAPAN

In 552 a Korean king sent missionaries to the islands of Japan. They carried to the Japanese court an image of the Buddha and a letter from the king, praising the religion as "the most excellent of all teachings . . . . It brings endless and immeasurable blessings and fruits, even the attainment of the supreme enlightenment . . . the Treasures of the glorious religion will never cease to give full response to those who seek for it."

The letter started a debate in Japan. If the foreign religion were accepted, would it offend the *kami? Kami,* the Japanese believed, were spirits that inhabited all nature. Simple shrines devoted to the *kami* dotted the country. Japanese mythology traced the ancestry of their emperor to the sun goddess, the most powerful of all *kami.* It was only after the introduction of Buddhism that these beliefs and practices were given a name—Shinto, or "the Way of the Gods."

One noble family adopted Buddhism and built a temple for worship. Unfortunately, soon afterward a plague broke out, and the new religion was blamed. The temple was ordered destroyed. However when the plague grew worse the Buddhists petitioned to rebuild their temple. The argument between the two sides went on.

In 592 Prince Shotoku Taishi became the chief adviser to the Japanese empress, Suiko. Shotoku, an ardent Buddhist convert, urged the empress to adopt the religion. Two years later Buddhism was proclaimed the state religion. Prince Shotoku began to build a temple complex as a center of Buddhist learning. This was the start of the structure later known as the Horuji, one of Japan's greatest Buddhist shrines.

TRANSFORMATION OF JAPAN

Japan sent envoys to China to study Buddhist scriptures and learn more about the religion. The mission found more than it had bargained for. It brought back Chinese ideas of culture and government, along with Confucianism and Daoism as well. From that beginning Japan began to adopt and adapt much that was valuable in Chinese culture, including Buddhism.

Prince Shotoku and his successors began to transform Japan. In 710 a new capital was built at Nara, a city modeled on China's capital, Chang'an. Many Buddhist monasteries were built within the city, and the emperor Shomu expressed his devotion to Buddhist dharma. In an imperial decree Shomu declared: "Our fervent desire is that, under the aegis of the Three Treasures (the Three Jewels), the benefits of peace may be brought to all in heaven and on earth, even animals and plants sharing in its fruits, for all time to come."

However, the Buddhist monasteries became so powerful and at times violent toward anyone who tried to stand up to them that the imperial family eventually had to move away to escape the oppressive atmosphere that had developed. This led to the founding of the next capital city of Kyoto in 794.

SHINTO MEETS BUDDHISM

Shomu's daughter, the empress Koken, took steps to unite Buddhism with Shinto. She arranged a ceremony for the Shinto god of war, Hachiman. Buddhist monks and nuns obediently prayed to this god—an unlikely one, since the Buddha preached nonviolence. The monks placed a cap on a sacred cart supposed to contain the spirit of Hachiman. In this ceremony both religions were given equal status in Japan.

The introduction of Buddhism was a spur to Japanese culture. It provided an outlet for the Japanese love of beauty. Buddhism, as the Hachiman ceremony showed, was also a flexible system that could adapt to different ideals, because it stresses the insignificance of things worldly. Indeed, not long after its introduction Buddhism in Japan would become the favored religion of the samurai warrior class and would be reflected in much of Japanese culture.

TIBET

Now formally part of China, Tibet, the "Land of Snows," is located in a large plateau of the Himalayas, often called the "Roof of the World." Because of its remote location Tibet has often been isolated from the rest of the world. The Tibetan indigenous religion,

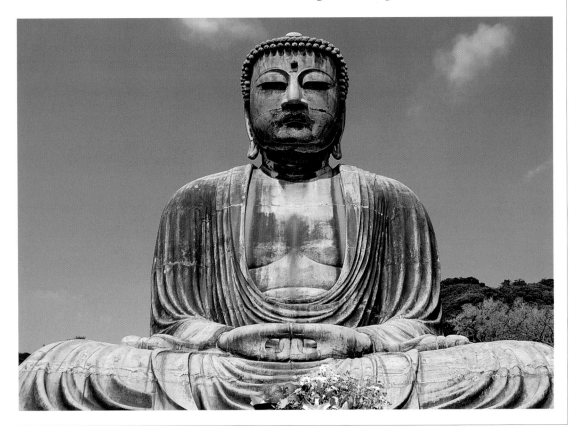

A bronze statue of Amida Buddha in Kamakura, Japan. The statue, which was cast in 1252, is more than 38 feet (11.5 meters) high and the second-largest Buddha statue in Japan.

known as Bon, was a mixture of magic and animism. The Bon-po, a type of shaman, or medicine man, recited mantras, sacred formulas or magical words used to exorcise evil spirits or to call forth powerful forces. In early times Bon-pos presided over the death rites of the Tibetan kings.

Buddhism first arrived in Tibet in the seventh century when a Tibetan king married a Chinese princess. She was a Buddhist and brought with her images for which the king built a temple. However Buddhism did not become strongly rooted until the arrival of the Indian Buddhist, Padmasambhava, a century later.

According to Tibetan tradition Padmasambhava, or Guru Rinpoche, encountered a series of demons as he made his way toward Tibet. The demons wanted to keep him from ending their hold on the country. Fortunately Padmasambhava possessed a knowledge of magic and overcame the demons. He did not destroy them. Instead Padmasambhava forced them to submit to the dharma and become the new protectors of the religion. The legendary defeat of the demons explains Buddhism's absorption

Flags covered with Buddhist prayers surrounding a temple on a mountaintop in Tibet. The prayer flags have been left by pilgrims; each flutter of the flag is regarded as a repetition of the prayer printed on it.

of local religious traditions in Tibet. Padmasambhava established the first Tibetan Buddhist monastery, Samye, completed in 779.

To this day Padmasambhava is a culture hero in Tibet, celebrated in dance and song. He brought not only the religion that is universally practiced but also the Tibetan written language. Buddhism became the single most important force in the lives of the Tibetan people. In the centuries that followed, an enormous number of monasteries and temples were built. From Tibet, Buddhism spread farther north into Mongolia.

DECLINE IN INDIA

Ironically, as Buddhism spread throughout Asia it was fading in the land of its birth. Hinduism was going through a period of regeneration. New schools won greater popular support. On his pilgrimage to India, Xuanzang noted that at Benares, where the Buddha had preached his first sermon, most of the people were Hindus. In some areas the Buddha was worshipped as a reincarnation of Vishnu, one of the Hindu trinity of chief gods. Only in the monasteries was Buddhism a vital force.

The final blow to Indian Buddhism came when Muslims from Afghanistan invaded northern India around the year 1200. They sacked and burned many shrines and monasteries. The great university at Nalanda was destroyed and the invaders fed its library to the flames for 10 days. The great era of Buddhism within its founder's homeland was over.

Today Buddhist monks live at some of the famous sites of the Buddha's life. They welcome pilgrims from the many lands where Buddhism has taken root. Though the message of the Buddha is still honored by millions of people in Asia, less than 2 percent of the population adhere to this faith in India, the land of his birth.

CHAPTER 4

THE VARIETIES OF BUDDHISM

The Buddha said, "The dharma which I have taught you will be your teacher when I have gone." Soon after the Buddha's death his followers gathered in a council to agree on his teachings. A century later a second council was held. By this time different viewpoints about the dharma had started to appear among the Buddhists. As Buddhism spread further and the community grew, two viewpoints took shape that have defined the different forms of Buddhism to this day.

One was a conservative approach that desired to hold as much as possible to the doctrines and practices as originally formulated. This approach was called the School of the Elders, or Theravada.

The other group chose to interpret liberally the teachings and practices of the Buddha. By the beginning of the common era its followers had given it the name Mahayana, which means "great vehicle." Buddha had referred to his teaching as a raft, a vehicle that carried pilgrims across the river to the "other shore." The name *Mahayana* conveyed the idea that it would carry the whole world to salvation. Mahayanans mockingly labeled the Theravada School as the "lesser vehicle," or Hinayana.

Buddhist monks belonging to the Theravada tradition meditating inside the shrine room of Wat Phra Singh in Chiang Mai, Thailand. The temple, or *wat,* was founded in 1345, although little of the original building remains.

The Bodhisattva Vow

The bodhisattva, or "being of wisdom," not only radiates compassion but even bears the pains and sufferings of others.

I take upon myself . . . the deeds of all beings, even of those in the hells, in other worlds, in the realm of punishment . . . I take their suffering upon me . . . I bear it, I do not draw back from it, I do not tremble at it . . . I have no fear of it . . . I must bear the burden of all beings, for I have vowed to save all things living, to bring them safe through the forest of birth, age, disease, death and rebirth. I think not of my own salvation, but strive to bestow on all beings the royalty of supreme wisdom . . . For it is better that I alone suffer than the multitude of living beings. I give myself in exchange. I redeem the universe from the forest of purgatory, from the womb of flesh, from the realm of death . . . For I have resolved to gain supreme wisdom for the sake of all that lives, to save the world.

—Basham (275)

What Have You Done

Think not of the fault of others, of what they have done or not done. Think rather of your own sins, of the things you have done or not done.

—From the *Dhammapada* (4:50)

MAHAYANA BUDDHISM

At the center of Mahayana Buddhism is the figure of the bodhisattva—literally, a "being of wisdom." A bodhisattva is a being who is very close to nirvana but turns back before reaching it to work for the salvation of all beings. A bodhisattva will delay entry into nirvana until even the smallest creature has reached the highest goal. The Buddha had been a bodhisattva in his lives (or rebirths) before he was born as Siddhartha Gautama.

THE SIX VIRTUES

The bodhisattva is a savior. A bodhisattva gains merit for humankind by practicing the Six Virtues, or *paramitas*. A virtue is practiced to perfection when it is carried out with a mind free from self-consciousness, ulterior motives, or self-praise.

The six virtues are:

1. The perfection of giving (*dana*)
2. The perfection of morality (*sila*)
3. The perfection of patience (*santi*)
4. The perfection of courage (*virya*)
5. The perfection of meditation (*dhyana*)
6. The perfection of wisdom (*prajna*)

Bodhisattvas can be reborn as humans or even animals. However the most powerful bodhisattvas are those in heaven. The Mahayana School of Buddhism developed the idea of a heaven peopled with bodhisattvas who could be adored and petitioned with prayer. The heavens also include past buddhas (enlightened ones) and a buddha of the future—Maitreya.

THE BODIES OF THE BUDDHA

The new development of the bodhisattva as an ideal raised a question about the historical Buddha. Why didn't he remain a bodhisattva instead of selfishly reaching nirvana and passing from existence? The Mahayana answer to this problem is found in a doctrine called the Three Bodies of the Buddha.

The Buddha's three bodies are the Body of Essence, the Body of Bliss, and the Transformation Body. Living on earth as Sid-

Devotional statues on the terrace of a temple in Hong Kong, China.

Some bodhisattvas have been more important or beloved than others. Among these are:

Maitreya, the earliest bodhisattva, around whom a cult of devotion formed. He answers the prayers of worshippers. A compassionate and benevolent being, he grants help to anyone who calls on him.

Avalokitesvara, who is rich in compassion and love because he has purified his vows for countless eons. He can take any form that will help human beings. He grants rewards and wishes to those who remember him and recite his name. He is the patron of Tibet; in China, where he was transformed into the female Guanyin, he is the most popular of all bodhisattvas.

Manjushri (meaning "sweet" or "gentle"), the symbol of wisdom and eloquence. He is young and never grows old. Manjushri usually appears in dreams, sometimes as an orphan or a poor man. Whoever worships him is protected by the power of Manjushri and is certain to reach enlightenment.

dhartha Gautama, the Buddha inhabited the Transformation Body. However his Transformation Body was really an emanation, or manifestation, of his Body of Bliss. In the Body of Bliss he dwells in the heavens eternally as what might be called a supreme god. The Body of Bliss in turn is an emanation of the Body of Essence, which is the Ultimate Buddha. The Ultimate Buddha underlies the entire universe and is identified with nirvana itself. The Ultimate Buddha, or Body of Essence, is much like the World Soul, or Brahman, in Hinduism presented in a new form.

A PANTHEON OF BEINGS

Mahayana theology developed the idea that there were other Bodies of Bliss—all emanations of the single Body of Essence. These Bodies of Bliss were identified as bodhisattvas and "other" buddhas who had lived at various times in past history. These figures multiplied into a pantheon of beings who dwelled in numerous heavens, hells, and even other universes. Mahayana Buddhist thinkers envisioned wonderful paradises and their counterpart hells, where the wicked suffered horrible punishments. The only limit to new creations was the human imagination.

The most beloved Bodies of Bliss were those concerned with life and sufferings here on earth. The most important were the Buddha Amitabha (Immeasurable Radiance), who resided in the heaven of the west. He was linked with the historical Buddha Gautama and the powerful and compassionate bodhisattva Avalokitesvara, whose name means "the Lord Who Looks Down."

DOCTRINE OF EMPTINESS

Mahayana theology was buttressed by two primary philosophical schools. The first school was the Madyamika, or Doctrine of the Middle Position. It was developed by Nagarjuna, who lived in the first and second centuries of the common era. Nagarjuna postulated that all that exists is emptiness, or the Void (*sunyata*). For this reason his theory is sometimes called the Doctrine of Emptiness. Nagarjuna admitted that for practical purposes the everyday world existed. However because it was composed of transitory or impermanent phenomena, it had no absolute reality. Since emptiness is the only phenomenon that never changes, the Void is absolute reality. The Void, in fact, is the same as nirvana and the Body of Essence of the Buddha.

The Madyamika doctrine included a very optimistic corollary. Although the existence of emptiness could not be proved by ordinary logic, it could be directly experienced in meditation. The emptiness, or Void, was everywhere; indeed there was no difference between the ultimate Void and the world of phenomena. Humans and all beings were already part of the emptiness or Void. Potentially they were all buddhas if they could only, through meditation, recognize the Void and realize the true nature of things.

The Madyamika doctrine was popular in China and Japan. Because it emphasized salvation in the real world, it appealed to the practical spirit of the Chinese and Japanese. Since the real world and nirvana were the same, Madyamika appealed to the love of nature that was an important value in both countries. Indeed portrayal of the Void became especially important in Chinese and Japanese art. Moreover the

Statue of Guanyin, the goddess of mercy and compassion, in the courtyard of a Chinese temple. The male bodhisattva Avalokitesvara was transformed in China into this female deity whose help is sought in times of need.

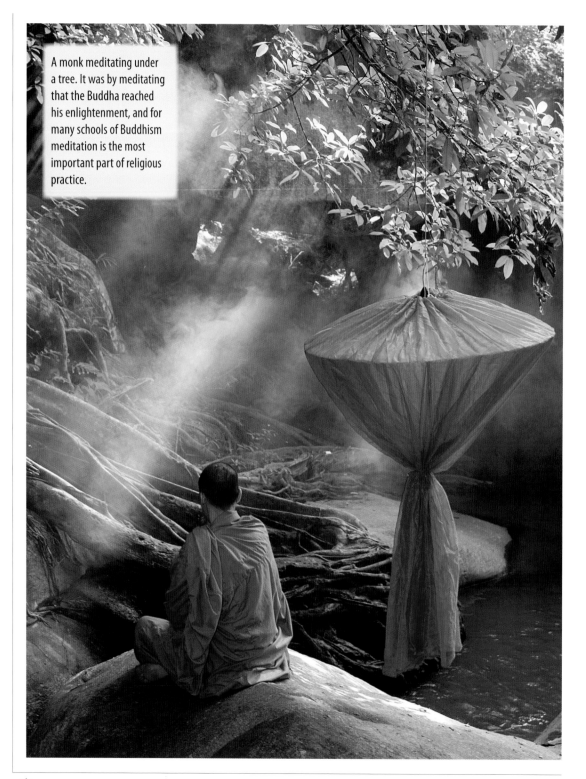

A monk meditating under a tree. It was by meditating that the Buddha reached his enlightenment, and for many schools of Buddhism meditation is the most important part of religious practice.

Madyamika doctrine offered a quicker path to enlightenment. The need for rebirths was less important, for nirvana or buddhahood were omnipresent and only needed to be realized.

YOGACARA SCHOOL

The second philosophical school, called Yogacara, was founded in the fourth century. Its central belief is that the phenomenal world exists only in the mind of the beholder. It uses as an example the monk who in meditation can conjure up visions that are as real as his ordinary perception of the mundane world. Yet the monk knows that they are a product of his own thoughts. The only independent reality outside the mind, according to the Yogacara School, is an entity called *suchness*. Suchness (*tathata*) is without characteristics, pure and whole. It is the counterpart of the Void of the Madyamikas.

Salvation in the Yogacara School came from purifying oneself until one reached the state of absolute purity, or suchness. The purifying process was a rigorous one, and only those at a high state of spiritual development could achieve it. Basically the meditating person conjured up visions that were as vivid as possible, absorbing their reality. Through constant practice the subjectivity of the perceptions of the everyday world and his visions would be apparent. The adept would realize that all phenomena were subjective. Only when the visions and ordinary phenomena were perceived in the same manner was suchness reached.

DIFFERENCES BETWEEN THERAVADA AND MAHAYANA BUDDHISM

Although both Theravada and Mahayana Buddhism recognized Siddhartha Gautama as the founder of the religion, their differences were profound. They can be summarized in nine points.

1. The ideal of the *arhat* and the ideal of the bodhisattva. In Theravada Buddhism the ideal was the *arhat*. The *arhat* was one, who through the Eightfold Path became an enlightened one and thus experienced nirvana. His aim was single-mindedly to reach enlightenment for himself. In Mahayana Buddhism the bodhisattva postpones personal nirvana to work for the salvation of all beings.

2. The goal of nirvana and the goal of buddhahood. In Theravada Buddhism the goal was to attain nirvana through the Eightfold Path. The goal for the Mahayana Buddhist was the attainment of buddhahood itself. The Theravadins recognized a difference between the achievement of the buddha, which was the highest possible, and the attainment of nirvana by an *arhat*. In Mahayana anyone could in theory reach buddhahood.

3. The role of self-effort and the role of faith in achieving the goal of salvation. The Theravadins stressed that nirvana can only be achieved through the efforts of the individual alone. Mahayana Buddhists permitted the use of prayers and faith, and the help of the buddhas and bodhisattvas, as part of the process of salvation.

4. The historical Buddha and many buddhas. The Theravadins stressed the importance of the historical Buddha, whose greatness lay in his dharma. Although they regarded him as the highest specimen of humanity, they did not regard him as divine. In Mahayana Buddhism the historical Buddha was one of many buddhas and bodhisattvas. He was identified with the Supreme Essence and thus had attributes of a god.

5. The monks and the laity. Theravada Buddhism has been called a religion of monks. The sangha was the center of the religious community. The laity gained merit through serving the sangha by providing food and donations in return for its precious teaching. In Mahayana Buddhism the sangha was important as a preserver and teacher of Buddhist tradition and learning. However the laity had a larger role: They could pray directly to the bodhisattvas and could seek salvation directly through them.

6. The importance of wisdom and compassion. The highest attribute of Theravada Buddhism is wisdom. The attainment of it brings nirvana. In Mahayana Buddhism the highest attribute is compassion—to bring the whole chain of being to salvation.

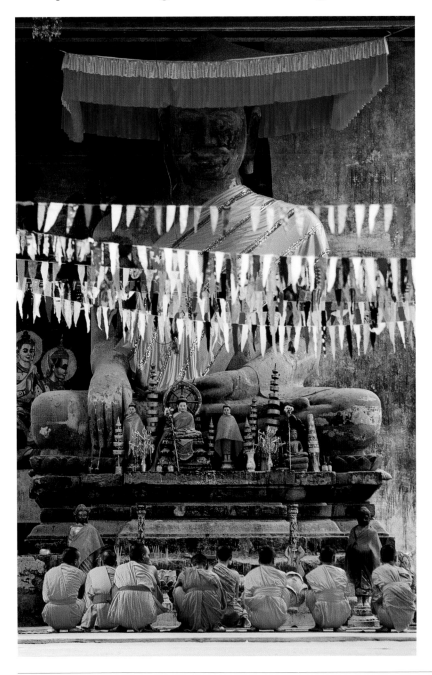

Novice monks belonging to the Theravada tradition of Buddhism meditating before a giant stone statue of the Buddha at Angkor Wat in Siem Riep, Cambodia.

7. Pali and Sanskrit scriptures. Both branches of Buddhism claim that their scriptures, or sutras, are the direct teachings of the Buddha, transmitted orally for generations before being written. The Theravada scriptures were first written down in Sri Lanka in the first century B.C.E. They are in Pali, an ancient Indian language. The Mahayana scriptures were written down later in the Sanskrit language. They contain some of the same literature as the Theravada texts but have an enormous library of their own. Mahayana Buddhists believe that their new cosmic sutras were given by the Buddha to specially chosen disciples, and these take place in astonishingly beautiful other worlds.

8. One school and many schools. Theravada has only one school of religious thought. Its followers claim that this is the same one that the historical Buddha taught in his lifetime. The Mahayana branch of Buddhism has many schools. Their liberal interpretation of Buddhism was more open to new schools of thought, which are constantly evolving.

9. Spread by southern route or northern route. The Theravada branch of Buddhism spread to the south. The countries of Sri Lanka, Myanmar (formerly Burma), Thailand, Laos, and Cambodia all practice Theravada Buddhism. Mahayana Buddhism arose in the northwest of India. According to tradition King Kanishka convoked a Buddhist council at which sutras were written down. Mahayana Buddhism spread from northwest India across Asia to China, Korea, and Japan.

THE PURE LAND TRADITION

When the Chinese first encountered Buddhism they had no idea of the split within it. They took the different scriptures as they obtained them, in pieces. As the Chinese pilgrimages to India show, the first phase of Chinese Buddhism included attempts to obtain as many texts as possible.

Later the Chinese made their own contributions to Buddhist doctrine. First Chinese scholars enriched the religion by adding commentaries to Mahayana scriptures. Xuanzang, for example, devoted himself to the Yogacara School and wrote commentaries, or interpretations, of its texts. Other scholars synthesized the many Mahayana writings into a single coherent system.

CHINESE METHODS OF DEVOTION

The Chinese also developed the Meditation School. In this tradition the techniques of meditation superseded the need for scriptures. These Chinese contributions were important because it was Chinese Buddhism that spread to Vietnam, Korea, and Japan—where new forms, traditions, and practices were subsequently added. However the Chinese contribution went beyond scholarly commentaries and techniques. Chinese religious leaders developed everyday methods of devotion that helped to make Buddhism a popular religion in East Asia. An example was the Pure Land tradition, which centers on the Buddha Amitabha.

THE PURE LAND

The paradise in which Amitabha dwells is called the Pure Land. In this place of splendor the leaves and flowers of the trees are precious stones of all colors. On its waters grow lotuses larger than any on earth. Birds sing continually, the clouds pour forth music, and chimes tinkle in the breeze from the trees. Those who follow Amitabha can someday reach this idyllic Pure Land.

In China, where Amitabha is called Amituofo, the Pure Land tradition developed in the seventh century. Devout Pure Land Buddhists believe that if they call on the name of Amitabha, he will lead them to the Pure Land after their deaths. This belief brought great comfort from the sufferings of the world. Over time the simple invocation of his name became the most popular religious practice in China. In religious art Amituofo was depicted sitting

BUDDHA AMITABHA

The Buddha Amitabha (the Buddha of Boundless Light) is one of the most beloved of the "new" buddhas of Mahayana Buddhism. Buddhists believe that in a former time, eons ago, when Amitabha was on the verge of enlightenment, he made a vow: When he had attained his goal, if there were any "beings in other worlds" who heard his name and thought upon him favorably, then he would help them. If he did not keep this vow, then he prayed that he would not attain enlightenment at all. Since Amitabha did in fact become a Buddha, the truth of his vow was assured. Thus people could call on his help at any time.

on his Lotus Throne, often flanked by Guanyin, China's favorite and ubiquitous bodhisattva.

HONEN AND SHINRAN IN JAPAN

The Japanese monk Honen (1133–1212) helped develop the Pure Land tradition in Japan. He returned there, after a long stay in China, during a time of turmoil when competing military leaders waged war on one another. Honen's answer to the disorder and suffering was total dependence on the compassion of Amida, the Japanese version of Amitabha, and all that was required for salvation was to call repeatedly on the name of Lord Buddha Amida.

Shinran, a monk and a disciple of Honen, carried his teacher's ideas further. He declared that expression of the phrase only once

The Buddha in a reclining position as he enters *parinirvana,* the final stage before nirvana, in the Jade Buddha Temple, Shanghai, China. This modern temple draws from both Pure Land and Chan traditions of Mahayana Buddhism.

in a lifetime brought salvation. In a shocking gesture Shinran took a wife, thus breaking his monastic vow of chastity. He argued that since the grace of Amida was all that mattered, the discipline of monastic vows was unimportant. He claimed that the family and the home were the proper setting for religious life. Shinran organized his followers into the True Pure Land tradition.

THE CHAN SCHOOOL

Another major school of Mahayana Buddhism that developed in China was the Chan, or Meditation, School. Meditation has always been important to Buddhism. The Buddha himself, sitting under the Bodhi tree, reached enlightenment through meditation. The Meditation School, however, found special meaning in Buddha's advice: "Look within, thou art the Buddha."

The arrival in China in 520 of Bodhidharma, an Indian missionary monk, launched the Chan School. By tradition Bodhidharma came to China to restore the original spirit of the religion. On his arrival he met the Chinese emperor, who described all the things he had done to promote the religion. The emperor asked Bodhidharma, "What merit have I earned from my acts?" Bodhidharma replied, "None whatsoever." The emperor then asked what Bodhidharma regarded as the first principle of Buddhism. "Vast emptiness," said Bodhidharma.

MEDITATION—TRUTH IN ACTION

Following the example of Bodhidharma, the Chan School of Mahayana Buddhism put meditation firmly at the center of its

Namu Amida Butsu

The call to Amida was not new to Japanese Buddhism. Honen, however, made it the essential element of his preaching. The repetition of the phrase namu Amida butsu ("Hail to Lord Buddha Amida") was all that was required for salvation. A text of the Pure Land Sect declares:

The mere repetition (of the phrase) with firm faith includes all the practical details. . . . Those who believe this, though they clearly understand all the teachings Shaka [the historical Buddha] taught throughout his whole life, should behave themselves like simple-minded folk, who know not a single letter, or like ignorant nuns or monks whose faith is implicitly simple. Thus without pedantic airs, they should fervently practice the repetition of the name of Amida, and that alone.

(In William Theodore De Bary, *The Buddhist Tradition in India, China, and Japan.*)

Bodhidharma's Meditation

After meeting the Chinese emperor in 520 the Indian missionary monk Bodhidharma retreated to a monastery, where he stayed for nine years. During that time he constantly meditated while staring at a blank wall. It is said that when his eyelids started to droop from fatigue, Bodhidharma cut them off and cast them aside. In the places where they fell tea plants grew. Tea's original popularity was as a stimulant that helped keep Buddhist monks awake during meditation.

Buddhist pilgrims, having climbed Jiuhua in winter, offer prayers and incense at the summit. Jiuhua is one of the four sacred Buddhist mountains of China.

religious practice. Meditation was not only a method or means of intuiting the Body of Essence, but the only way. Indeed meditation was more than a means—it was believed to be the truth realized in action. In pursuit of this goal followers felt free to give up the study of scripture to pursue an intuitive approach to enlightenment. The techniques of meditation were passed from master to disciple in a completely personal transmission of insights.

The Chan School was influenced by the two indigenous Chinese philosophies. Confucianism and Daoism taught that humans were basically good. People only needed guidance and support to tap their essential wisdom. Confucius taught that people should keep their minds on the here and now. Daoists taught that people should follow their own nature. "Everything is what it is," and understanding this was a form of enlightenment. To increase intuition Daoists had often used riddles and paradoxes. Chan Buddhism combined this technique with a down-to-earth outlook. In addition, in a break with tradition, the monks were required to perform physical labor.

The Meditation School spread to Korea and Vietnam, but it had its greatest influence in Japan. Known there as Zen, it combined the mystic conceptions of the Indian version with the down-to-earth approach and techniques of the Chinese. The goal was to use meditation to reach *satori,* or enlightenment. Zen Buddhism had two main schools, Rinzai and Soto. Both were transmitted to Japan in the 12th and early-13th centuries.

RINZAI SCHOOL

Eisai (1141–1215) was a Japanese monk who was discouraged by what he considered the staleness of religion in Japan. He journeyed to China for further study and there became attracted to Chan. After achieving enlightenment Eisai returned to Japan as a Zen master. He set up his school, called the Rinzai, and soon attracted disciples. The Rinzai used koans (Japanese for *gong'an*) as an aid to cleansing the mind for meditation. Thinking about them could bring one to the state of readiness for *satori*. Eisai claimed for his doctrine, "Outwardly it favors discipline over doctrine, inwardly it brings the Highest Inner Wisdom."

Dogen (1200–53), the second founder of Japanese Zen, established the Soto School. Dogen's followers used *zazen* meditation as the way to reach *satori*. *Zazen* was sitting (*za*) meditation (*zen*).

SHARED BELIEFS AND PRACTICES

Both Zen traditions, Rinzai and Soto, shared many beliefs and practices. Each revered the historic Buddha. In both the training went from a master to his disciples. Each sect believed that within each person it was possible to awaken the Buddha mind. Both argued that religious devotion was expressed in daily work.

Zen became the religion of the warrior class in Japan. The warriors, or samurai, were attracted by a religion where it was not necessary to study philosophical texts or to observe ritual. It was simple and emphasized discipline, a trait honored by the warrior. Zen was also the inspiration for many of the distinctive arts of Japan.

TANTRIC BUDDHISM

Around the fifth century C.E. a new variety of Buddhism arose in India, called Vajray-

KOAN *(GONG'AN)*

The Chinese Meditation School developed the koan. This was a paradoxical statement to shake up the mind. A master would tell his pupils puzzling tales whose point was obscure. Or the master might pose a series of seemingly unanswerable questions. (An example is, "What is the sound of one hand clapping?") While the pupil meditated on these stories or questions, masters would often do something to shock them. They might shout into the pupil's ear or even give them a sharp blow with a stick. The purpose of this was to jolt the pupil into a state that embraced both the world of meditation and the physical world. Combining them both at once would make the pupil aware of the true nature of things. They would thus achieve the suchness goal of Yogacara philosophy.

Sitting Meditation

A follower of Dogen described the process of *zazen*, sitting meditation:

In a place, which must be quiet, spread a thick cushion and sit yourself on it in an upright posture. Now first swell out the abdomen and put your strength there. Let the shoulders be in a straight line below the ears, and navel below the nose. Make the spine straight. The mouth should be shut, but you may have the eyes slightly opened. Making the breath flow gently will help you to secure a correct posture. Then meditate on the text you have been given, or in the case of beginners there is a method in which they count their breaths and so remove dull and distracted thoughts. So entering the Samadhi or undisturbed purity, remain in the meditation.

(In Edward Conze, I. B. Horner, and D. Snellgrove, *Buddhist Texts through the Ages*.)

ana, or Tantric Buddhism. The two names reveal the unusual nature of its relationship to Mahayana Buddhism. The word *Vajrayana* ("the thunderbolt" or "diamond vehicle") implies that it is a whole new branch of Buddhism. The thunderbolt is a symbol of Ultimate Reality, or the Void. However Mahayana philosophy underlies Vajrayana, although the latter used a new technique to attain salvation—the tantra.

Tantra is the name for manuals or guidebooks that contain the techniques for gaining enlightenment. The tantras included magic spells (mantras), occult diagrams (mandalas), and symbolic hand gestures (*mudras*).

REACHING A MYSTICAL REALITY

Tantric methods were practiced by Hindus and Buddhists alike. Their goal was to reach a mystical union with reality beyond everyday reality. This was symbolized in Hinduism as the union between a god and his consort. In Buddhism the union was between bodhisattvas or buddhas and a feminine partner. Through meditation the devotee reached an inner unity with the Buddha or bodhisattva and experienced bliss and Ultimate Reality. Someone who was adept in tantric practices in Tibet was called a lama. It is not necessary for a lama to be a monk.

MARPA AND MILAREPA

In the 11th century a Tibetan guru, Marpa (1012–96), renewed the Tantric tradition after studying in India. Marpa was a married householder who led the ordinary life of a farmer. Yet he translated the Sanskrit writings of Buddhism and gathered disciples to whom he revealed the secrets and practices of tantrism he had learned in India. Spiritually he claimed descent of the teachings from a buddha called Vajradhara ("Holder of the Vajra").

Marpa's most famous disciple was Milarepa (1040–1123). For many years Milarepa meditated in caves in the high Himalaya Mountains, practicing and developing the techniques he had learned from Marpa. His powers included the ability to develop internal heat so that even in the bitterly cold winters of the world's highest mountains, he wore only a thin robe of white cotton.

Neither Marpa nor Milarepa was ever ordained as a monk. They were important in Tibetan Buddhism for creating poetry to express their personal religious experiences. This began a tradition that has continued in Tibet to modern times.

GELUG-PA SCHOOL

Toward the end of the 12th century waves of Indians entered Tibet fleeing the Muslim invaders who devastated northern India. Before this time Tibetan pilgrims had gone to India for spiritual learning. Now Tibetans began to see their own country as the spiritual center of Buddhism. They believed that the Buddha himself had prophesied this destiny. The bodhisattva Avalokitesvara began to be revered as the patron of the Tibetan state.

In the 15th century a religious leader named Tsongkhapa established the Gelug-pa School. It was important for two reasons. First, the Gelug-pa became the dominant school in Tibetan Buddhism. Tsongkhapa founded monasteries near Lhasa, the capital, and made that city the center of his religious group.

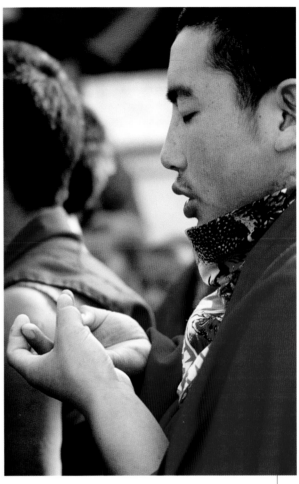

A Tibetan Buddhist monk chanting and making a *mudra* in Dharamsala, northern India. *Mudras* are symbolic hand gestures used in images of the Buddha; they are also used in ritual meditation to help focus the mind, especially in Tibetan Buddhism.

Second, the line of Dalai Lamas became established.

THE DALAI LAMA

The third successor of Tsongkhapa was the first Dalai Lama ("Ocean of Wisdom"). He and his successors are believed to be reincarnations of Avalokitesvara. For centuries afterward, on the death of the Dalai Lama, a search began for the child who was his latest incarnation. Once found, the child was educated by the elder

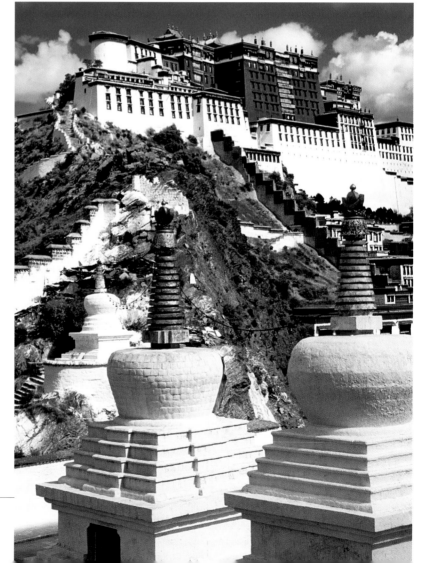

The Potala Palace in Lhasa, Tibet, was the winter palace of the Dalai Lama from the 17th century C.E. This was the chief residence of the Dalai Lama until 1959, when the Chinese took control of Tibet. The Dalai Lama escaped to Dharamsala in northern India, where he set up a government-in-exile, and thousands of Tibetan Buddhist refugees have since joined him. The Potala Palace has been turned into a state museum by the Chinese but continues to draw thousands of Tibetan pilgrims as well as international tourists. It was declared a World Heritage Site by UNESCO in 1994.

LAMA

Vajrayana became part of the Buddhism of Nepal, China, and Japan. However its greatest development and elaboration took place in Tibet. By tradition the Indian monk Padmasambhava introduced Tantrism to Tibet. In Tibet a guru was called a lama. A lama need not be a monk—his skills in the tantra were all that mattered. The lama assumed such importance in Tibet that the religion is sometimes called Lamaism.

The highest duty of the lama was to guide a dying person as the spirit left his or her body. For 49 days the spirit would exist in *bardo*, the state between after death and rebirth. During this time the instructions given by the lama would help the spirit reach either enlightenment or rebirth.

lamas in preparation for his role. In 1642 a converted Mongol chief placed the Dalai Lama on the throne of Tibet, making him both the temporal and religious leader of the country, a position that endured until 1959, when the Chinese Communist government took control of Tibet. Lamaism, or Tibetan Buddhism, despite the exile of the Dalai Lama, is still the religion of more than 65 percent of the Tibetan people. A revival of Tibetan Buddhism also began in Mongolia in the 1990s.

CHAPTER 5

THE LITERATURE OF BUDDHISM

Near the summit of Mount Kaya in Korea, nestled amid cascading mountain streams and a grove of trees, is one of Buddhism's most famous shrines—the Haeinsa Temple complex. "The impermanence of all things" is marked by the brief appearance of cherry blossoms in spring and the brilliant foliage of flaming maples and golden oaks in the fall. Thousands of visitors come each year to the 93 wooden structures that include a monastery where monks chant Buddhist sutras day and night.

Yet the most important part of the Haeinsa Temple is its library, housed in two buildings that are more than 600 years old. They contain more than 80,000 wooden blocks that were originally used to print copies of the Buddhist scriptures on rice paper.

The blocks were carved on the order of King Kojong of Korea in the 14th century. At the time Mongol invaders occupied his country, and the king sponsored the project to ensure divine

A Buddhist pilgrim spins a prayer wheel at Swayambunath Stupa in the Kathmandu Valley, Nepal. Prayer wheels containing scrolls of scriptures are spun during Buddhist devotions. As the wheels are turned the prayers are multiplied.

favor for the Koreans. Over a 16-year period a total of 81,258 woodblocks were completed. Each birch woodblock, carved on both sides, measures about nine by 27 inches.

The Koreans succeeded in driving out the Mongols, and the precious woodblocks were housed in the Haeinsa Temple, near today's city of Taegu. Because the wood was specially treated to prevent decay, the blocks have survived to the present day. They make up the world's largest single collection of Buddhist scriptures.

PRESERVING THE BUDDHA'S TEACHINGS

As followers of the Mahayana tradition, the Koreans preserved its written forms. However, even this vast collection contains only part of the complete Buddhist canon. Theravada and Mahayana Buddhism have some scriptures in common. However as Mahayana Buddhism spread, its literature greatly expanded. Today the combined writings of the many Buddhist traditions are more extensive than those of any other world religion.

Buddhism never had a single book such as the Bible or the Quran that all its believers accepted. Many schools of Buddhism concentrated on just one scripture as their guide, but later schools have added their own scriptures. Certain works, however, even if in different languages and slightly varied forms, are beloved by all Buddhists.

For 500 years after the death of the Buddha his followers memorized and recited his teachings. After the *parinirvana* the sangha met to agree on the teachings of the Buddha. They preserved them orally, even though India had a written language, for in the Indian tradition the actual speaking of the sacred words had a special value. The fact that most of the canon was in verse form and used standard opening phrases made memorization easier.

As the years passed and differences crept into the religion, there was a greater need to commit the Buddha's teachings to writing. The first written Buddhist scriptures were recorded on palm leaves shortly after 43 B.C.E. in Ceylon (present-day Sri Lanka). Written in the Pali language, they became the scriptural basis for Theravada Buddhism. They are called the Tipitaka, which means "three baskets," as the texts, which were divided into three categories, were often literally stored in baskets.

THE THREE BASKETS

The first basket is the Vinaya Pitaka, or "Basket of Discipline." These writings concern the sangha. They give the Buddha's rules of discipline for the monks and nuns. In addition they provide information on the founding and history of the early monasteries.

Handwritten Tibetan Buddhist scriptures from the Mahayana tradition and prayer beads that are used to focus the mind during devotions.

The second part of the Tipitaka is the Sutta Pitaka, or "Basket of Discourses." This basket includes the *suttas* (sutras in Sanskrit), or sermons and stories of the Buddha and his earliest disciples. In these the Buddha describes his doctrine and the practices necessary to reach nirvana. The Sutta Pitaka contains many of the most popular works of Buddhism.

This second basket includes the Theripatha—songs of devotion by the first Buddhist nuns. The Theripatha is the world's earliest collection of sacred poetry by women. Among its authors was the Buddha's aunt, his foster mother, Mahaprajapati.

The third basket is the Abhiddhamma Pitaka, or "Basket of Metaphysics." It contains commentaries on the teachings of Buddhism.

THE LOTUS SUTRA

Later—by tradition at a council called by King Kanishka in the second century C.E.—Mahayana Buddhists collected their writings in Sanskrit. Called the Tripitaka, this collection is divided into the same categories and contains some of the same works as the Tipitaka. However, the Mahayana Buddhists maintain that the Tripitaka contains doctrine that the Buddha revealed only to his most spiritually advanced followers.

Among the important works in the Mahayana Tripitaka is the Lotus Sutra. Its author, supposedly the Buddha himself, employs a wealth of images and parables to teach its message. One story is similar to the biblical parable of the Prodigal Son. The theme of the Lotus Sutra is universal salvation and the attainment of buddhahood by all believers. In East Asia many Buddhists believe that the *Lotus Sutra* embraces and harmonizes the full spectrum of Buddhism.

"Lamp Unto Yourself"

One of the most popular works of Buddhism contained in the Sutta Pitaka is the last sermon of the Buddha, called "Lamp Unto Yourself." It concludes:

Therefore, O Ananda, be ye lamps unto yourselves. Be ye a refuge to yourselves. Betake yourselves to no external refuge. Hold fast to the truth as a lamp. Hold fast as a refuge to the truth. Look not for refuge to anyone besides yourselves . . .

(In Aphonso-Karkala, *An Anthology of Indian Literature.*)

THE JATAKAS

Among the most beloved works found in both the Tipitaka and the Tripitaka are the Jataka Tales. In these stories the Buddha tells about his former lives. By tradition the Buddha recalled all of his 550 previous states of existence while he attained enlightenment under the Bodhi tree.

Some of the most charming Jataka Tales describe his adventures in earlier rebirths when he took the form of an animal. The Buddha used these tales to explain his doctrine simply. The Jataka Tales remain popular today and have inspired Asian drama and art for centuries.

Each story begins with an event that caused the Buddha to relate it. In "The Hare Jataka" the Buddha and 500 of his followers arrive at the home of a devout layman, described as "a landowner of Savatthi." For seven days the landowner treats them to the hospitality of his house. At the end of the week the Buddha praises the landowner for his generosity, saying that the "wise men of old lay down their lives for the beggars they met." Asked to tell about the past, the Buddha begins the tale.

A hare lived in a forest at the foot of the mountains, next to a river and a small town. The hare had three companions: an otter, a jackal, and a monkey. By looking at the moon the hare saw that the next day would be a holy day. He taught his companions that they should fast and prepare to give food to any passing beggar.

The next day the otter went to the river and smelled a string of seven red fish that a fisherman had buried in the sand. The otter dug them up and asked loudly, "Does anyone own these?" However since the fisherman had gone downstream no one answered, and the otter took the fish to his lair, saying, "In due time I'll eat them."

The jackal found in the hut of a field watchman two spits of meat, a lizard, and a pot of milk. He too called for the owner, but when no one appeared he dragged them back to his lair, thinking, "In due time I'll eat them."

The monkey picked a bunch of mangoes from a tree in the forest and placed them in his lair, saying, "In due time I'll eat them."

The hare went out and thought to gather grass to eat. However he realized that if a beggar came by grass would not be a sufficient meal. "I have no rice nor oil," thought the hare. "So if a beggar comes to me I will give him my own flesh."

This resolution was so virtuous that it warmed the throne of Sakka in heaven. He disguised himself as a Brahmin and went to earth. First he came to the otter, who offered him the seven red fish. The Brahmin promised to come back on the next day. Then he went to the jackal, who offered the meat, lizard, and milk. Again the Brahmin said he would return. The same thing happened at the monkey's lair.

Finally the Brahmin came to the hare. The hare said, "You did well in coming to me for food. For I will give a gift that I have never given before. However you, as a moral man, will not have to take life. Go and make a fire and when it is ready I will leap into it and when my body is roasted you may eat my flesh."

The Brahmin used his supernatural powers to make a fire. The hare remembered that there might be insects in his fur, so he shook himself three times so that they would not be killed. Then he jumped into the fire. However he lay there as if he had entered a cave of snow.

"Brahmin," said the hare, "the fire you have made isn't even able to heat the fur on my body. How is this?"

"Wise man, I am not a Brahmin. I am Sakka come to test you."

The hare said, "Your efforts are useless, for if all the beings in the world would test my generosity, they would not find me unwilling to give."

"Wise hare," said Sakka, "let your virtue be proclaimed to the end of the world-cycle."

Sakka took a mountain and squeezed juice from it and with the juice carefully drew the outline of a hare on the moon. Then he placed the hare on a nest of soft grass and departed for his celestial abode.

The hare and his friends lived happily and virtuously and passed away according to their deeds.

Having finished the tale, the Buddha revealed that in this existence the otter was Ananda, the jackal and monkey were two of his other followers, and the hare "was I myself." (Adapted from *Stories of the Buddha*.)

THE WAY OF RIGHTEOUSNESS

No Buddhist scripture is more widespread than the *Way of Righteousness* (the *Dhammapada* in Pali; the *Dharmapada* in Sanskrit). It is a source of wisdom and comfort to all Buddhists. The *Way of Righteousness* is a selection of the brief sayings that the Buddha made during his 45 years of teaching. There are 423 verses

THE *DHAMMAPADA*

Selections from the 423 verses contained in the *Dhammapada*, one of the most widespread Buddhist scriptures:

1. All that we are is the result of what we have thought: it is founded on our thoughts, it is made up of our thoughts. If a man speaks or acts with an evil thought, pain follows him, as the wheel follows the foot of the ox that draws the carriage.

2. All that we are is the result of what we have thought: it is founded on our thoughts, it is made up of our thoughts. If a man speaks or acts with a pure thought, happiness follows him, like a shadow that never leaves him.

129. All men tremble at punishment, all men fear death; remember that you are like unto them, and do not kill, nor cause slaughter.

135. Not nakedness, not plaited hair, not dirt, not fasting, or lying on the earth, not rubbing with dust, not sitting motionless, can purify a mortal who has not overcome desires.

277. "All created things perish." He who knows and sees this becomes passive in pain; this is the way to purity.

278. "All created things are grief and pain." He who knows this becomes passive in pain; this is the way to purity.

arranged in 26 chapters under such topics as friendship, thought, earnestness, punishment, and evil.

A PHILOSOPHICAL EXCHANGE

The conversion of King Milinda by Nagasena was a milestone in the spread of Buddhism. It also produced an important text of Buddhist literature—the *Milindapanha,* or "Questions of Milinda." The *Milindapanha* is written as a dialogue between the two historical figures. King Milinda asks Nagasena to explain puzzling or difficult Buddhist ideas. Nagasena's answers, often in story form, are used by Buddhist teachers today to illustrate key points of the dharma. For example:

King Milinda asked, "Why are people different in their natures? Some are long-lived, sickly, ugly or weak, while others are the opposite."

Nagasena's response is used to explain karma. He replied: "Why is it that all vegetables are not alike, but some sour, and some salty, and some pungent, and some acetic, and some astringent, and some sweet?"

"I fancy, sir, it is because they come from different kinds of seeds."

"And just so, great king, are the differences you have mentioned among people

A novice monk in Myanmar (formerly Burma) offering devotions in front of a statue of the Buddha in a reclining position. This position represents the Buddha entering *parinirvana* just before his final release at nirvana.

THE BURNING HOUSE

To illustrate the principle of using "lesser vehicles" to help all living beings, the Buddha relates the Parable of the Burning House.

Buddha asked Sariputra to imagine an old and wealthy man who owns a great house. The house is old, "the bases of its pillars rotten, the coverings and plaster of the walls loose." It has only one door. Within live the man's many small children.

One day the house catches fire and the owner escapes through the door. However he realizes that the children inside are not aware of the danger. The owner wishes to save them. Because he is strong he considers carrying them through the door. However the door is small and it may be difficult to gather the children together, for they are running around in all parts of the house.

Instead the householder calls out to them, warning of the danger. However they do not heed his cries, for they are too young to understand even the meaning of "burning."

The householder knows that the children love to play with toys. So he tells them that he has three toy carts outside for them to play with. Hearing this, they rush toward the doorway, each trying to be the first one through it.

Outside, however, the householder gives them something different. He is a rich man and gives each of them a real cart drawn by bullocks and swift as the wind. He thinks, "Why should I give these children inferior carts, since they are precious to me?"

"Now, Sariputra," asked the Buddha, "is that man guilty of a falsehood by first holding out to his children the prospect of three vehicles and afterward giving each of them only the greatest vehicles?"

"No," answered Sariputra, "for it was only a skillful device to persuade his children to go out of the burning house and save their lives."

The Buddha replied that the householder is like the Buddha himself, who found a way out of this world of suffering and pain. Having saved himself, he wished to save his children as well. However they are ignorant and think of enjoying themselves in the world. So he tells them of the three lesser vehicles. Attracted by them, the children will acquire the knowledge of the Four Noble Truths—the one single grand cart that will take them to nirvana.

to be explained. For it has been said by the Blessed One: 'Beings, O Brahmin, have each their own Karma, are inheritors of Karma, belong to the tribe of their Karma, are relatives by Karma, have each their Karma as their protecting overlord. It is Karma that divides them up into high and low and the like divisions.'"

THE LOTUS SUTRA

The Saddharma-Pundarika, or The Lotus of the True Law, is one of the most important sutras of Mahayana Buddhism. In it the historical Buddha teaches a disciple named Sariputra. The sutra is a justification of the additional features of Buddhism that appeared in the Mahayana forms of the religion. Among these are the "lesser vehicles" such as the bodhisattvas.

The acceptance of these "lesser vehicles" as part of Buddhism is one of the differences between Mahayana and Theravada Buddhism. Theravada followers teach only the Buddha's original, stricter dharma, the "Great Cart" of the parable. The Mahayana author of the Lotus Sutra has the Buddha justifying the use of "lesser vehicles" as a way to assist all living beings toward spiritual perfection, or buddhahood.

CHINESE DEDICATION MESSAGES

Buddhism flourished in China for more than 200 years during the Tang dynasty. Scholars developed new Buddhist schools of thought, which acquired distinctively Chinese features. Philosophical disputes, however, offered little to the ordinary person. As in the Lotus Sutra, people were attracted to Buddhism by "lesser vehicles," although the essential spirit of the Buddha persisted.

One way a person could gain merit was by paying to have copies made of the scriptures and sutras. In many of the copy texts a dedication message explained the motivation of the person who paid for it. These messages show the meaning and comfort Buddhism brought to ordinary Chinese. Here is an example of a dedication message written by a monk at the request of a Chinese Buddhist called Madame Tuan. She would have paid the monk to

The wheel of dharma, the way and teachings of the Buddha, on the roof of a temple. In early Buddhist art the Buddha himself was not represented and symbols such as a wheel, the Bodhi tree, the footprints of the Buddha, or a riderless horse were used instead.

write part of a sutra and asked that her dedication be put at the beginning of the scriptures:

The lay disciple Madame Tuan (née Chang) has ever lamented that the fragrant orchid, like a bubble, blooms for but one day, and that separation from loved ones causes so much sorrow. She wonders how it can be that heaven feels nothing for the calamities it inflicts and causes the worthiest to be the first to be cut down, just as the young tree is the first to wither and the highest blossoms are the first to fall.

Thus, on behalf of her deceased third son, Commissioner Tuan, an officer of the local commandery, she has reverently had a section of the Golden Light Sutra copied. Now that the transcription is completed she prays that her son's spirit may visit the blue heavens, that he may mingle with the immortals, that he may travel in person to the Pure Regions and listen to sutras being recited under the tree. She also prays that he may never pass through the three unhappy states of existence or the eight calamities, but will gather karma sufficient to enable him to proceed joyfully to the Lotus Palace and the Flowering Throne, that he will never again suffer a short life but enjoy longevity in the Pure Land and may be perpetually reborn only there.

His loving mother, thinking of him, prays that the karma for both of them may be good and that they may both enjoy the fruits of salvation.

ZEN STORIES

In Zen Buddhism disciples received their training from a master who already had experienced enlightenment, or *satori*. A Zen master might actually beat his students with a wooden sword to shock them out of their ordinary ways of thought. Usually this tactic worked. The master knew as well how to illustrate the principles of Zen through surprising actions and speeches. Anecdotes about the great Zen masters are among the cherished texts of this form of Buddhism:

Joshu asked the teacher Nansen, "What is the true Way?"
Nansen answered, "Everyday way is the true Way."
Joshu asked, "Can I study it?"

Nansen answered, "The more you study, the further you are from the Way."
Joshu asked, "If I don't study it, how can I know it?"
Nansen answered, "The Way does not belong to things seen: nor to things unseen. It does not belong to things known: nor to things unknown. Do not seek it, study it, or name it. To find yourself on it, open yourself wide as the sky."

PREPARATION FOR DEATH

An excerpt from the Tibetan Book of the Dead:

(The Lama speaks to the dying person): *I now transmit to you the profound teaching which I have myself received from my Teacher . . . Pay attention to it now, and do not allow yourself to be distracted by other thoughts! . . . If you suffer, do not give in to the pain! . . .*

The factors which made up the person known as (the name of the dying person) *are about to disperse. Your mental activities are separating themselves from your body, and they are about to enter the intermediary state. Rouse your energy, so that you may enter this state self-possessed and in full consciousness!*

First of all there will appear to you, swifter than lightning, the luminous splendor of the colorless light of Emptiness, and that will surround you on all sides. Terrified, you will want to flee from the radiance . . . Try to submerge yourself in that light, giving up all belief in a separate self, all attachment to your illusory ego . . .

If you miss salvation at that moment, you will be forced to have a number of further dreams, both pleasant and unpleasant. Even they offer you a chance to gain understanding . . . But you must know that all you perceive is a mere vision, a mere illusion, and does not reflect any really existing objects. Have no fear, and form no attachment! . . .

Three and a half days after your death Buddhas and Bodhisattvas will for seven days appear to you . . . Wonderful and delightful though they are, the Buddhas may nevertheless frighten you. Do not give in to your fright! Do not run away! . . . Pray to them with intense faith and humility, and, in a halo of rainbow light, you will merge into the heart of the divine Father-Mother, and take up your abode in one of the realms of the Buddhas.

THE TIBETAN BOOK OF THE DEAD

An important ritual in Tibetan Buddhism takes place when a person is dying. In the Vajrayana tradition, after death a person enters a 49-day intermediary state (*bardo*) between the end of one life and the beginning of another. At this time a person who is properly prepared can attain nirvana. If that does not happen he or she will remain on the cycle of rebirth.

The Book of the Dead is a spiritual manual that assists the lamas in preparing the dying person to seize this important opportunity to end the cycle. Different texts of the manual exist.

CHAPTER 6

THE ARTS AND BUDDHISM

From Afghanistan to Japan, from India to Indonesia, Buddhism has been a major influence on Asian art. Buddhism interacted with many national traditions to produce artworks and architecture of incredible variety. The richly gilded shrines and temples of, for example, the Temple of the Gold Buddha (Wat Traimit) in Bangkok, Thailand, represent one ideal. The unfinished wood and simplicity of a Japanese Zen monastery represent another. This chapter will present only a small sample of the Buddhist artistic heritage.

THE IMAGE OF THE BUDDHA

In the earliest Buddhist art the figure of the Buddha was not shown. "On the dissolution of the body beyond the end of his life," reads a Buddhist text, "neither gods nor men shall know him." The historical Buddha, after his *parinirvana*, had passed into invisibility; thus it would have been inappropriate to create his human image. Instead the Buddha was indicated only by symbols—the Bodhi tree, an empty throne, footprints, a wheel, or a riderless horse.

Trashi Chhoe Dzong (monastery) at Thimpe in Bhutan is the religious and political center of this Himalayan kingdom. Buddhism is the state religion of Bhutan and this monastery houses the offices of the king and the throne room.

By the beginning of the common era that artistic convention began to change. In the centuries since, the image of the Buddha has played as important a role in Asian art as that of Christ did in the art of Europe. Asian artists worked to express the qualities of enlightenment in physical form. Buddhism provided a stimulus for art of the highest spiritual order.

Images of the Buddha sitting on a lotus throne in a temple in Ho Chi Minh City, Vietnam. The lotus plant has a deep symbolic significance in Buddhism. The roots of the plant are embedded in the mud under water, but the flower blooms above the water. In the same way, the Buddha lived in a corrupt world but kept his purity and clarity.

The earliest depictions of the Buddha only appear around the beginning of the first century C.E. There were two different styles. In Gandhara in the northern part of the vast Kushan Empire, the style reflected the Greco-Roman heritage. This had been one of the areas conquered by Alexander the Great and long colonized by Greeks. Buddha was dressed in robes that were draped in Greek fashion. His head was sculpted with wavy hair, and he wears a toga. It is this style that has dominated the usual image of the Buddha ever since.

Another style, influenced by Hindu art, appeared in Mathura in the very south of the Kushan Empire. The Mathura Buddhas were clothed in a light Indian dhoti, or long skirt. The hair was straight and tied in a topknot. Molded out of sandstone, these images were closer to Indian sculpture styles, with soft, gentle curves. The Buddha is smiling gently. From these two traditions the classical Buddhist image arose. It has certain characteristics that make it immediately recognizable in spite of different national and ethnic traditions.

LAKSHANAS, ASANAS, AND *MUDRAS*

The Buddha's holiness is also indicated by marks called *lakshanas*. It was believed that the Buddha had 32 *lakshanas,* which were signs that he was an enlightened one. The one most often seen in his portrayals is the halo that surrounds either his head or whole body. Called the *prabhamandala,* it indicates his divinity. The topknot or protuberance (*the ushanisha*) on top of his head signifies the super brain and supreme wisdom that Buddha attained at his enlightenment. Finally the *urna,* or mark on the forehead, is a sign of spiritual insight. On some statues the *urna* may be inset with a precious stone.

The Buddha figure was portrayed in various positions, or asanas, appropriate for teaching, blessing, or meditation. His hand gestures (*mudras*) were also conventionalized. The right hand held palm outward with the fingers pointing upward is a teaching gesture. The hand position signifying deep meditation shows the hands on the lap, palms up, with the right hand over the left.

STYLES OUTSIDE OF INDIA

Images of the Buddha spread beyond India. In China the earliest Buddhist art was influenced by the Gandhara style. These Buddhas were done in gilt bronze with heavy concentric folds in the robes. Instead of the traditional seminudity of Indian gods and goddesses, Chinese sculptures were covered by scarves, shawls, and skirts. In time the image of the Buddha in East Asia took on a distinctly Chinese appearance.

In many Asian sites Buddha statues are hewn out of rock faces, such as the huge Buddha at Sokkuram Grotto in Korea and the Bamiyan Buddha in Afghanistan. This mammoth Bamiyan Buddha was carved out of a cliff and signified the Buddha Vairocana, the cosmic and omnipresent Buddha. The statue's immense size indicated his role as savior of the world. In 2001 the Taliban regime of Afghanistan ordered the destruction of the statue, one of Afghanistan's pre-Islamic treasures. Countries around the world protested the order, but the statue was reduced to rubble. A priceless part of Afghanistan's Buddhist history was lost forever.

The Reclining Buddha of Sri Lanka is also of enormous size. This position represents the Buddha's death, or *parinirvana*. Unique to Thailand are walking Buddhas, some with undulating arms that represent another of the Buddha's asanas, the resemblance of his limbs to the trunk of an elephant.

Whatever the pose, the Buddha figure has brought out the best in Asian artists. Most of these works were done by anonymous Buddhist monks whose sculpting was an act of devotion. The growing pantheon of bodhisattvas and Buddhas heightened the inspiration for the art.

THE IMPORTANCE OF THE STUPA

Buddhist architecture started very simply with the stupa. A stupa is a mound-shaped structure first used to cover the ashes and

SOKKURAM GROTTO

The Korean Buddha at Sokkuram Grotto, on Mount Toham, is one of the great achievements of Asian art. Carved entirely from the rock face of the mountain, a towering Buddha gazes outward toward the sea. The Buddha is seated in the Pose of Enlightenment. His legs are folded in the lotus position, the left hand lies palm up in the lap, and the right hand rests palm down on the right knee. The morning sun glints off a jeweled *urna* on his forehead. The pose was designed to create a spiritual experience in the viewer.

relics of the Buddha. The early stupas were constructed of mud bricks and subject to disintegration. In appearance these structures were simple and uninspiring. Still the stupa remained the basic architectural design of Buddhist temples. As a circular structure it resembled—in three-dimensional form—the wheel of the dharma.

Over time stupas became more elaborate. The mound that held the relic increased in size. Its summit was often flattened, with the top enclosed by a railing. This high place represented the heaven of the gods who governed the visible world. Frequently an umbrella (or a series of umbrellas) rose above it, symbolic of royal power—the power of the Buddha and his dharma.

GREAT STUPA AT SANCHI

The most important early stupa is at Sanchi in central India. The Buddha never visited Sanchi, but Asoka did. It was the site of the monastery from which Asoka sent Mahinda to Sri Lanka to convert that country to Buddhism. Asoka's wife, Devi, founded the monastery and her husband later started the stupa to commemorate his bringing the dharma to Sri Lanka. The original stupa measured about 60 feet (18.2 meters) in diameter and about 25 feet (7.6 meters) in height.

Over time the Sanchi stupa was doubled in size and its older wooden railings were replaced with massive nine-foot-high stone balustrades. (These are today covered with the names of pilgrims who have visited over the centuries.)

To strengthen the dome of the stupa it was covered with stone blocks and topped with a three-tiered umbrella. The three levels of the umbrella represented the Three Jewels of Buddhism: the Teacher (Buddha), the Law (dharma), and the community of

THE GREAT BUDDHA AT TODAIJI

A Buddha Vairocana, representing the omnipresent Buddha, was created in Nara, Japan. In the eighth century the Japanese emperor asked for contributions for this Buddha to fulfill a vow made when an epidemic of smallpox swept the country. The casting of the bronze image was an enormous task. Standing 53 feet (16 meters) high and weighing more than 200 tons, it was gilded with 500 pounds (227 kilograms) of gold. Taking pride and joy in their achievement, the Japanese dedicated the statue in the Todaiji Temple in 752, exactly 200 years after Japan received its first image from Korea. At the dedicatory ceremony—called the "eye-opening"—the Great Buddha was presented to the people in the grandest celebration Japan had ever seen.

monks (sangha). Four magnificently carved gateways, each 34 feet (10.3 meters) high, faced the four points of the compass. The square columns depict events from the life of the Buddha and his previous lives—a sculptured representation of the Jataka.

STUPA AT BOROBADUR

The largest stupa in the world is on the island of Java in Indonesia. Java was visited by traders and missionaries and settled by Indian colonizers, who brought to the island both Hinduism and Buddhism. In the eighth century Java became the center of a sea-going empire governed by the Sailendra ("King of the Mountain") dynasty. The Sailendra kings were ardent Buddhists and under their patronage the island experienced a flowering of culture. The greatest achievement of the Sailendras was the Borobodur, whose name means "Monastery of Accumulated Virtue."

The giant stupa at Borobodur symbolizes the Mahayana Buddhist view of the universe and consists of six square terraces surmounted by three circular terraces. The stupa is symbolic of the Mahayana Buddhist view of the universe. At the lower levels sculpted reliefs show humans bound to the cycle of rebirth. Higher up are beautiful scenes from the life of Siddhartha Gautama. Various bodhisattvas are also portrayed. Carved in the upper circular terraces are images of the Buddha in contemplation. At the very top is a huge, undecorated stupa. It represents the eternally unseen and unseeing—the Void, or nirvana.

CHINESE PAGODAS

In China the stupa evolved into the pagoda, a tall, multistoried tower. Chinese pagodas are octagonal in shape and

A "WORLD MOUNTAIN"

The great stupa at Sanchi in central India is the most important early historical stupa. By the fifth century C.E. the early brick dome of the Sanchi stupa was completely transformed into a "world mountain." At the base of the stupa sat four images of the Buddha, facing each of the gates. The tiered umbrella symbolically joins heaven with the earth through the huge dome.

No one could enter the stupa itself, for it was completely sealed. The stupa was not a place to house worshippers, but an enclosure for relics of the Buddha. Traditionally Buddhists paid homage at holy sites by walking around them (circumambulation). At Sanchi a stone walkway was built around the stupa at a height of 16 feet (4.8 meters) above the ground. A staircase enabled worshippers to reach it.

always have an odd number of stories, ranging from three to 13. Like the Indian stupas, they enclose Buddhist relics. After Buddhism was accepted in China pagodas sprang up throughout the country. Built from brick, stone, and wood, thousands have survived, often being the only remaining structure from a long-gone monastery. One of the most impressive is the Big Goose Pagoda, built around the middle of the seventh century, standing in the former Chinese capital of Changan (today's Xi'an).

The stupa at Sanchi in Madhya Pradesh, India. Today, around 50 historic Buddhist and Hindu monuments remain at Sanchi and are visited by tourists from all over the world.

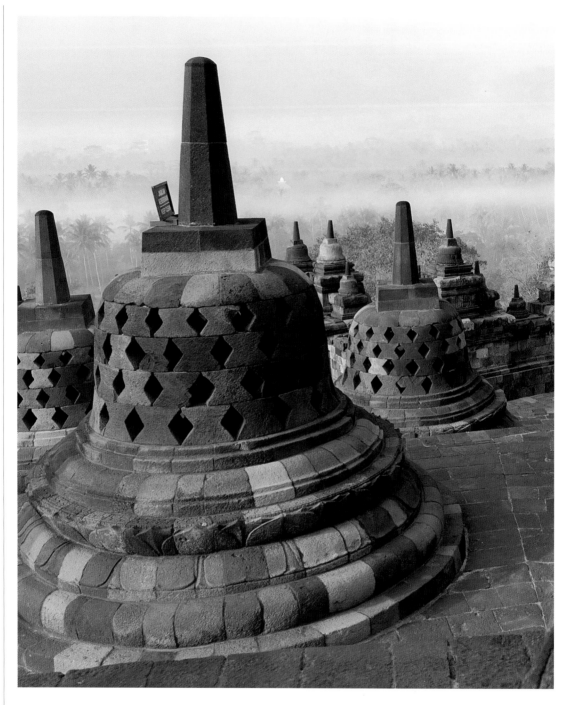

Small stone stupas on the terraces of the giant stupa at Borobadur, Indonesia.
The entire stupa shows in stone the path humankind can follow to reach nirvana
according to the Mahayana tradition.

The spread of Buddhism from China to Korea, Vietnam, and Japan brought with it the multistoried pagoda architectural style. By the seventh century C.E. pagodas were found in all three countries. They were often part of complexes that included study centers and a building or hall for worship. The worship hall was constructed to foster a sense of religious feeling. Usually it had an enormous roof over its high, spacious interior. Yet the light was not too bright, so that one had the proper sense of awe for the large image of the deity. Outside, leading to the worship hall, was a ceremonial gateway decorated with images of the guardian deities of Mahayana Buddhism.

BURMESE PAGODAS

In Myanmar (formerly Burma) the top of the stupa became elongated into a distinctive spire. One of the most beautiful examples is the Shwedagon temple at Yangon (formerly Rangoon). The temple contains eight sacred hairs of the Buddha.

Building pagodas took on a unique urgency in Burma. After King Arawrahta seized the Buddhist scriptures from the Mon city of Thaton around 1060, he brought them back to his capital, Pagan, in jeweled cases on white elephants. He started building pagodas to demonstrate his religious piety. The laity, rich and poor alike, were inspired to join the effort so they could gain spiritual merit, or good karma.

From the year 1044 to about 1300 Burma's kings and commoners went on a frenzy of building. An 11th-century stone dedication tablet describes a king who paid six oxcarts of silver for artisans to build a pagoda in his name. Kings were demanding in their standards. One threatened to execute a bricklayer if a needle could be inserted between the bricks of the pagoda. Price was no object, for Pagan became prosperous through trade with India and Sri Lanka.

MONASTERY COMPLEXES

At the same time that stupas and pagodas were spreading through Asia, developments were taking place in another kind of building:

In the space of 250 years, 5,000 pagodas were built at Pagan in Myanmar (Burma), creating a veritable forest of towers on the plain where the city stands. The total works out to about two pagodas each month. All were different—some ornate, some simple, large and small. Many were lavishly decorated with wall paintings and sculptures. Pagan's enormous effort was unprecedented in history.

The frantic construction came to an end when the Mongol chief Kublai Khan defeated the Burmese in battle. Pagan never regained its former political greatness. Over time many of the pagodas deteriorated or were destroyed. Even so, about 2,000 remain today, a ghostly reflection of the city's past greatness.

the Buddhist monastery. This structure consisted of prayer halls (*chaityas*) and living quarters (*viharas*) with individual cells for the monks.

Sometimes these halls and chambers were not built of wood or stone but hewn out of large rock formations. Rock-hewn architecture appealed to the Buddhist monks for several reasons. First, it was durable and stable. Second, such a dwelling continued the tradition of hermits and ascetics living in caves. Third, the cave mountains were located in secluded areas. The carved mountain became the perfect sanctuary for Buddhist monks.

CAVE MONASTERIES

Some of these stone-hewn constructions grew to an immense size. Looking at these giant architecture-sculptures today, the visitor is amazed to realize that they were excavated by monks who carved the cliff face away inch by inch. First an overall plan was devised. Then the sculptors carved the facade by cutting a rough opening that ultimately became the finished ceiling. This permitted them to work back and down through hundreds of square yards of solid stone and eventually to the chamber floor. The unwanted rock was removed and then the rock still embedded in the earth was shaped into rough forms by using iron picks. Finally the finishing was done with hand chisels.

CHAITYA AND *VIHARA* DESIGN

A stone stupa was placed within the *chaitya* hall. The *chaitya* hall is a long chamber divided by two rows of columns. In a rounded end, or apse, the two aisles meet and curve around the stupa, which holds relics and treasures of the monastery. The *viharas*, or monks' quarters, were generally designed as open square halls approached by a doorway through a porch. The doorway was encircled by small cells for the monks carved deeper into the rock. Here members of the sangha lived, meditated, and slept in close proximity to their prayer hall and the stupa. As the priestly community increased more cells were excavated farther away.

In the course of time small study rooms were added. Eventually a complex monastery was created. It consisted of the common room, a refectory, a kitchen, a tank for the water supply, and cells. The monasteries were centers of Buddhist learning and great Buddhist art.

AJANTA CAVES

The cave monasteries were particularly noted for their wall murals. The greatest of the Indian murals are at Ajanta in the southern region of India known as the Decca. Located on a high bluff near the town of Aurangabad, the caves sheltered monks as early as 200 B.C.E. Of the 30 caves that have been discovered, five

Looking across the pagodas of Pagan, Myanmar, at sunset.

are *chaityas*, or chapels for worship, and the rest are *viharas* where the monks lived. The site was abandoned by the year 650 C.E. and not rediscovered until 1819.

The glorious Ajanta murals were inspired by both major traditions of Buddhism—Mahayana and Theravada. From floor to ceiling the walls swirl with color and form. The stone was prepared by applying a series of surfaces, ending with a thin coat of white plaster. After the paint was applied the murals were polished to give them a luster that the centuries have only slightly diminished. Even in the dim light the Ajanta paintings shine with strong, vivid colors.

The subject matter is a breathtaking record of the Buddha's life and teachings. One immense painting of the reclining Buddha preparing for his *parinirvana* is angled to catch the sun from the mouth of the cave. The moving shadows play across the Buddha's face, which seems to change expression in the light. In addition, the artists depicted scenes from royal and upper-class

View of the Ajanta Caves, near Aurangabad, India. In addition to the many images of the Buddha and scenes from his life, the caves also display scenes from the Jataka tales. Other legends are illustrated, such as the temptation of the Buddha by the beautiful daughters of Mara and the legendary incident when the Buddha, taunted by an unbeliever, took the shape of a thousand buddhas to convince him of his divinity.

Indian life—probably to commemorate the patrons who sponsored the sangha that flourished in the caves. Scholars have found these to be a treasure trove of information about Indian life of the period.

TIBETAN ARTS

The art of Tibet is almost entirely religious, used for the ceremonies and traditions of Tantric Buddhism. The most common form of art is the painted banner (*tanka*). The *tankas* are hung inside temples and at family altars; they are carried by lamas in processions and used to illustrate sermons. Besides the Buddha, the subject matter of the *tankas* includes other Buddhas, bodhisattvas, and famous lamas. The Buddha often holds a thunderbolt, symbolic of the Tantric tradition, or a bell, which symbolizes the Void. Another tradition of Tibetan painting is the mandala, a geometric figure—usually a circle inside a square—that is regarded as the "dwelling of the god." At the center is a figure of the Buddha or another divinity. Surrounding it are fantastically intricate symbols and depictions of other gods and religious scenes. The object itself is used to gain supernatural powers. Some mandalas are constructed in sand or even on butter for specific ceremonies, after which they are destroyed.

Tibetan sculpture not only uses butter but also precious metals and other more permanent substances. Huge images are placed in the temples, and smaller ones on family shrines. The devout carry miniature images with them as "pocket shrines." Whatever the size of the image, it contains a cavity in the back that is filled with rolls of prayers or sacred relics. These are placed within the figure at a ceremony conducted by a lama. (The contents are sometimes called "sacred intestines.")

Tibetan art has also produced numerous ritual objects, the most famous of which is the prayer wheel. This is a round metal case or cylinder that revolves on a stick. Mantras, or prayers,

DUNHUANG CAVES

The largest surviving source of early Chinese painting is at the Caves of the Thousand Buddhas at Dunhuang. The walls contain pictures of all stages of the Buddha's life. All the favorite buddhas and bodhisattvas of the Chinese Mahayana faith are included. Artists here also portrayed vivid images of the different heavens on the way to nirvana. Even Xuanzang appears in scenes that show the hardships of his pilgrimage to India.

are either engraved on the cylinder or placed inside on paper. By turning the cylinder a person can gain the same merit he or she would earn by reciting the mantra—except, of course, the cylinder can be rotated more quickly than reciting the words aloud.

ZEN ARTS

Zen Buddhism had a very important influence on Japanese arts, which took on many of the aspects of the sect itself. Zen arts share the values of simplicity, austerity, purity, and an emphasis on the calm that comes from meditation. One can see this in the typical Japanese Buddhist monastery. It is constructed of plain unfinished wood with whitewashed plaster. There is no sculp-

A Tibetan Buddhist monk in the process of making a mandala while on a teaching and study tour in Vancouver, Canada. By meditating on the mandala, a person can attain clarity and insight.

ture, for worship of the Buddha has been de-emphasized. The whole panoply of Mahayana Buddhist figures is absent. At the center of the monastery is the meditation hall. The library, such an important part of other sects' monasteries, is less important, for the Buddhist scriptures also have been de-emphasized. The architecture is simple and functional.

TEA CEREMONY

One unique Japanese form that arose in the 16th century was the tea ceremony. By tradition Eisai, who brought Rinzai Zen to Japan from China, also brought tea. He advocated tea drinking for health and to keep oneself alert during meditation. Over time an elaborate tea ritual developed in which each movement in preparing, serving, and drinking tea is rigidly prescribed.

In a simple wood building the participants enter through a low door. By this act they humble themselves. Within there is little furniture or decoration except a beautiful object, such as a flower or tree sprig, in an alcove and a low table around which the participants are served tea. The tea and the utensils in which it is brewed and served are spare and simple. Each action, from the pouring of boiling water to the drinking, is choreographed. It is believed that the simple, ritualized movements help the participants cleanse their minds for contemplation.

SIMPLICITY AND EMPTINESS

Zen also affected Japanese painting. In keeping with the de-emphasis of the Mahayana hierarchy of Buddhas and bodhisattvas, there were no religious scenes. Instead Zen painters produced portraits of Zen masters. These simple, realistic, and psychologically acute portraits are among the greatest ever produced.

However, Zen ideas influenced secular as well as religious art. Most important, the Doctrine of Emptiness (the Void) inspired artists to "show by what is not shown." Japanese painters do not fill canvases or paper with brushstrokes. Much of the space occupied by the painting is empty—at least to the eye. The mind fills it in with what the artist has suggested.

The most famous Zen garden in the world is at Ryoanji Temple in Kyoto, Japan. It contains no living thing; 15 carefully placed rocks rest on white raked sand. This abstract design is a garden that involves the mind and invites meditation.

Zen also influenced gardens. The Japanese had been influenced by the Chinese view of a garden as a world in miniature. The essential elements of Chinese gardens were rocks (implying mountains), water, and plants. The Japanese took this a step further by simplifying the elements even more.

"THE TRUE FLOWER"

Although the Noh theater uses many elements of ancient Japanese drama, it strives for a Zen goal. Its objective is to portray meanings that go beyond words. In slow movements that resemble a dance, the masked actors tell stories of universal appeal. However in true Zen fashion Noh drama teaches more through intuition than statement. The test of judgment for a Noh performance is whether it possesses "the true flower."

"The true flower" is a reference to Siddhartha Gautama himself. A story about the Buddha tells of an occasion when he was seated around pilgrims who had come to hear him preach the law. The Buddha held up a flower in silence. The crowd was mystified except for Kashyapa, who looked at the flower and smiled inwardly. Buddha saw that he had understood "that which goes beyond the word." Kashyapa became the first of the 28 Great Patriarchs—the last being Bodhidharma, who brought the Meditation School from India.

GRASPING THE INNER SPIRIT

The Zen Buddhist tradition infused the painting style known as *sumi-e*. Artists used only black ink and a brush to produce subtle shades from light gray to black. Often the picture consisted of little more than swirls—which, however, suggested much more. "It takes only one blade of grass to show the wind's direction" was a Japanese saying.

Other artists used the "flung-ink" style to give the art a feeling of spontaneity. The goal was to grasp the inner spirit of the subject, creating a world of suggestion rather than explicit forms.

CHAPTER 7

THE YEAR IN BUDDHISM

As midnight approaches on the last day of the year men, women, and children gather at the Buddhist temple of Chionin. Here, in the ancient Japanese city of Kyoto, monks prepare for the ceremonies that will usher in the New Year. Exactly at midnight a group takes hold of a huge log and strikes the end of it against a bell 108 times. The deep sound reverberates throughout the city again and again. At each of the strokes of the bell the monks recite one of the frailties of humankind.

Children come forward with strands of rope, lighting one end at the temple flame. They will take the burning ropes home to rekindle the kitchen fire and light the candles at the household shrines. This is the day for beginning again, a time of hope and renewal.

Traditionally, in the days before New Year people have paid their debts, cleaned their homes, bought new clothes, and exchanged gifts to start the year with a clean slate. The ceremonies are tied to the Buddhist ideas of rebirth and purification.

Though the New Year begins on different days of the year in Buddhist countries with lunar calendars (based on the moon's

Novice monks holding alms bowls, ready to leave their temple in Myanmar (Burma) to go on their daily alms round to collect food and temple offerings from the nearby lay community.

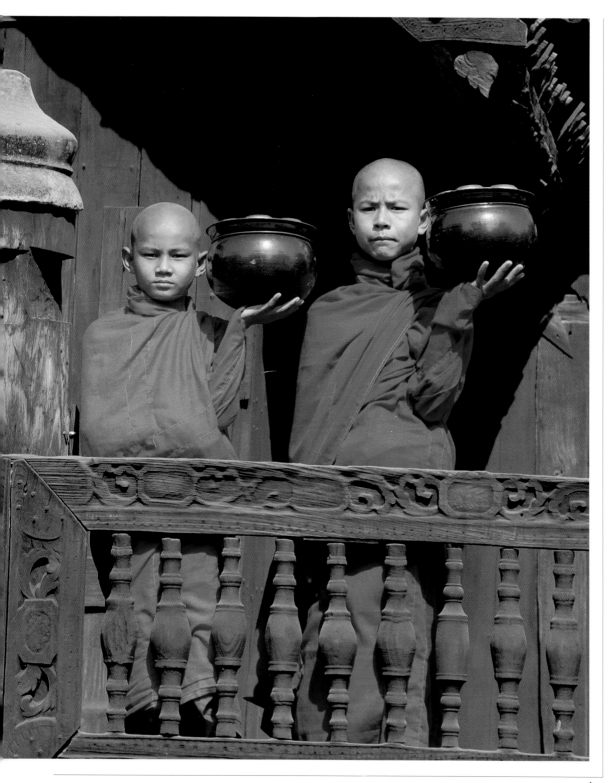

phases), people everywhere mark it in their own fashion. Frequently the New Year Day is a nationwide holiday on which no work is done, and people spend the time feasting, dancing, singing, and playing games.

Each form of celebration is influenced by local and national customs and varies according to the Buddhist tradition of that region. In addition to New Year the birth, death, and enlightenment of the Buddha are celebrated in all traditions, although these may occur at different times in the lunar calendar. The open and flexible spirit of the Buddhist religion embraces many forms of ritual and devotion.

RITES OF PASSAGE

The practice of Buddhism does not, strictly speaking, require a temple or the intercession of a monk. Anyone can follow the teachings of Buddhism in his or her daily life. The temples provide a refuge for those who wish to devote themselves more deeply to the teachings of the Buddha. Members of the sangha, however, are frequently called on to participate in ceremonies marking important events in people's lives—birth, marriage, and death.

BIRTH

Customs vary from country to country. In most Theravada countries, when a child is born its parents take it to the local temple to be given a name. The baby is blessed by the monks and sprinkled with holy water. A wax candle is lit and tilted on its side so that the drops of molten wax fall into a bowl of water. This ceremony symbolizes the coming together of the four elements: earth, air, fire, and water.

MARRIAGE

At some Theravada marriage ceremonies the young man and woman go to the local temple with their friends and relations. A long cotton thread is wound around the image of the Buddha and then around all those present. Symbolically united in one community, the congregation chants and the chief monk gives his blessing. Then the monk cuts two pieces from the thread and winds one around the wrist of the groom. The groom winds the other around his bride's wrist—monks are not supposed to touch women. However, in some Buddhist countries monks do not attend weddings, because it is regarded as bad luck.

FUNERALS

Monks have a special role at Buddhist funerals. When a member of a household dies a monk is summoned to recite special sermons and the sutra of the dead. However, funerals often involve a mixture of religious traditions and practices, with the Buddhist element only one of perhaps two or three different ritual aspects. For example, in China Daoist prayers and a belief in ancestors are as important as the monks' prayers for a good reincarnation.

Death rites commonly continue for a number of days, during which the bereaved family invites monks to eat in their household. This is done in order to transfer merit to the dead person, in case he or she has not accumulated enough good karma. Some families commemorate the death at another meal three months later and on the first year's anniversary of the death.

RELIGIOUS OBSERVANCES

Buddhists are not required to attend regular services at a temple, as Christians do on Sunday or Jews on the Sabbath (Friday night to Saturday). Nor do Buddhists have specified daily times of prayer as Muslims do. But in Theravada Buddhism devout laypersons may observe a "sabbath" called the *uposatha*. This falls on the 1st, 8th, 15th, and 23rd days of the lunar month. The faithful bring offerings to the temple on these days. Some may observe the day by remaining in seclusion to meditate and use the temple for this purpose. Others may listen to religious sermons. On these days the monks at the temple usually organize special rites that can include music, processions, and even firework displays.

During the monsoon season that comes at differing times from June to October in Southeast Asia, Buddhists observe a time of penitence that is the equivalent of Christian Lent. During this season monks observe stricter religious duties. This rainy period is a time of monastic retreat called Vassa during which many young boys or adults may take temporary ordination. Laypersons also increase their donations to the sangha and accumulate merit by meditating and listening to sutras.

VASSA

The rainy season is the time for an important religious observance called Vassa, or "Rain Retreat." This is the time when young people may choose to enter the sangha. In most Buddhist countries every boy over the age of seven is supposed to enter the sangha at least temporarily. He lives in the monastery for about two weeks for a vigorous religious training. In some countries it is also common for adult males to enter the sangha temporarily at this time to accumulate merit for themselves.

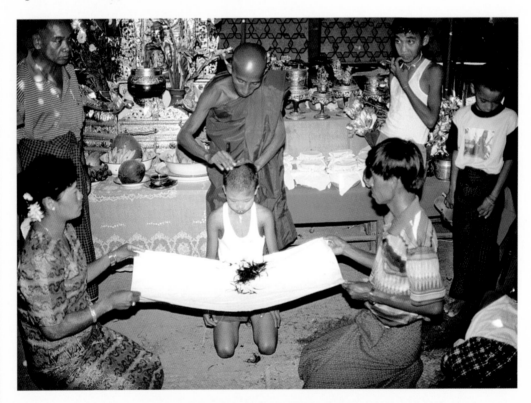

A Burmese boy having his head shaved on taking temporary ordination as a novice monk at the beginning of the month of Vesakha, the start of the rains.

This tradition may be the oldest one of the religion. It dates from the time when the Buddha himself, along with his disciples, wandered through northeastern India preaching the dharma. The rainy season, which in the nations of Southeast Asia is severe, required that the Buddha and his followers seek a place of refuge while it lasted.

FESTIVALS CELEBRATING BUDDHISM

In many Buddhist countries events in the life of the Buddha are commemorated at different times of the year. On these days people visit a temple bringing offerings of incense, cloth, flowers, and money. Often more elaborate celebrations involve everyone in the local community, much as Christmas is celebrated in predominantly Christian countries.

FESTIVAL OF LIGHT

In Southeast Asia the end of the three-month rainy season and the period of retreat called Vassa is celebrated in special ways. Theravada Buddhists in Southeast Asia, for example, celebrate Tavatimsa, which commemorates the Buddha's return to earth from heaven. According to tradition the Buddha ascended to the Tavatimsa heaven, one of the realms of existence, during Vassa and passed on the teachings to his mother. Many villages and towns are decorated with oil lamps, candles, and electric lights that burn all night long. The lights symbolize the enlightenment that the Buddha brought back to earth.

VESAKHA PUJA

In Thailand, Cambodia, Laos, and Sri Lanka the Buddha's birthday, enlightenment, and passing into nirvana are believed to have fallen on the same day in different years. In the Theravada calendar this is marked at Vesakha Puja on the full moon day of the second month of lunar year. (The festival is also known by names such as Baisakh Purnima in Nepal and Buddha Purnima in India.) People gather at temples to pay homage to the Buddha with lights, candles, food, and other offerings. Colorful processions walk around the temple three times in honor of the Buddha, dharma, and sangha and listen to sermons on the Buddha that can last the whole night. Streets and houses are lit with lamps to symbolize the Buddha's enlightenment, scenes from Buddhist stories are reenacted, and caged birds and caught fish are set free as acts of compassion.

The ceremony of placing paper boats containing offerings on streams and lakes during the Japanese festival of Obon stems from a Buddhist story that is much beloved in Japan. A young man named Mokuren had a dream of his mother in Gaki, the Hell of Starvation. Spirits were punished there by having lavish feasts set before them, but when the spirits raised the food to their mouths it turned into flames.

Mokuren, the story goes, asked the Buddha how to redeem his mother from this torment. The Buddha advised him to practice purity and kindness and to study the sutras. Mokuren became a *bhikkhu* and after many years dreamed that he had accumulated enough merit to set his mother free. In gratitude he set out a wondrous feast for the villagers. This was the first Feast of Obon.

HANA MATSURI AND OBON

In Japan Buddhists celebrate Hana Matsuri, the Buddha's birthday, on April 8. Traditionally people pour tea over the images of the Buddha in temples and homes. Special Zen holidays also occur at different times of the year. Some of these, such as Bodhidharma Day, commemorate important figures in the history of Zen.

A very popular Japanese holiday is the Feast of Obon. On this day, by tradition, the souls of the dead come to mingle with the living. People invite their neighbors and friends for an all-night feast. At dawn the living place little paper boats—holding candles, fruit, and flowers—in a nearby stream or lake. The boats carry off the souls of the dead.

ESALA PERAHERA

One of the most colorful Buddhist celebrations takes place in Kandy, a city in Sri Lanka. The Temple of the Tooth in Kandy houses the most precious of Sri Lankan Buddhist relics—a tooth of the Buddha that was found after his cremation. The relic is enclosed within seven jeweled caskets that are never opened. However, in August, on the feast of Esala Perahera, a replica of the innermost casket is carried through the torchlit streets on the back of an elephant magnificently outfitted with an ornamental covering. Crowds of pilgrims come for the occasion.

ARRIVAL OF THE DHARMA

In the Himalayan kingdom of Sikkim, where the Tantric form of Buddhism is dominant, a joyful and colorful celebration takes place in May. This is the anniversary of Padmasambhava's arrival in Tibet with the dharma. Brightly costumed "demons" gather in the streets, once more trying to chase Padmasambhava away. A lama wearing a fierce-looking mask takes the role of Padmasambhava and uses his magical techniques to vanquish the demons. Leading the triumphal procession are lamas wearing semicircular yellow hats that are also a badge of authority in Tibet, Mongolia, and Nepal.

LIFE WITHIN THE SANGHA

From the beginning the sangha—the orders of monks and nuns—have occupied a special place in Buddhism. While the Buddha was alive he established the sangha so that people could devote themselves fully to his Middle Way.

In the Theravada community the only way for devout members to attain nirvana is to enter the sangha, for only through the monastic life can one completely follow the Eightfold Path. For that reason it is common to place young boys in a monastery. At the age of eight they can receive a lower form of ordination called "the Going Forth." The child is dressed in his best clothes and carried to the monastery by his father; friends and relatives join the procession.

RECEIVING A MONK'S POSSESSIONS

At the door, in imitation of the Buddha, the child casts off his clothing and receives his novice robes. His head is shaved and he is given the begging bowl and the other possessions of a monk. As a novice he will be placed in the care of two monks. One will be his companion, the other his teacher. The novice prostrates himself before the companion and announces his intention to take refuge in the Buddha, the dharma, and the sangha. During their time at the monastery the young novices are taught the Ten Precepts that they must try to follow. These are some of the monastic rules set down by the Buddha, which are known as the Vinaya.

> **The Path to Wisdom**
>
> *If a person when young and strong does not arise and strive when he should arise and strive, and thus sinks into laziness and lack of determination, he will never find the path of wisdom.*
>
> —From the *Dhammapada* (20:280)

TAKING ORDINATION

The young novices are also taught the two cardinal virtues of wisdom and compassion, and that nothing should be believed just because it is a tradition or it is said by a teacher. A novice who chooses to stay will receive a final ordination at the age of 20. The Buddhist ordination ceremony is formal and impressive. It can only be performed by a group of at least 10 monks. The novice must request ordination three times, giving the name of his teacher and requesting anyone who opposes his ordination to speak. He receives a new name and three garments, including an outer and an inner robe as well as a cloak. Thereafter he must follow a stricter code of more than 220 rules, called the Pratimoksa.

The procedure and ceremonies for becoming a Buddhist nun are similar. If the novice is under 20 or has been married for more than 12 years, she must serve a probationary period of two years. Depending on the tradition a nun's garments include a robe or tunic and skirt and a belt.

THE TEN PRECEPTS

Novice Buddhist monks are taught 10 precepts, or rules. They are:

1. To refrain from taking life
2. To refrain from stealing
3. To refrain from sexual activity
4. To refrain from lying
5. To refrain from intoxicating substances
6. To refrain from eating after midday
7. To refrain from the use of perfumes and personal adornment
8. To refrain from seeing public entertainment
9. To refrain from grand beds
10. To refrain from accepting gold or silver

MONASTIC LIFE

A typical large monastery includes a monks' hall, where the members sleep in individual cells, and a sangha hall where they gather to eat, read the sutras aloud, and conduct meetings about monastery business. There may also be an inner hall where images of the Buddha and bodhisattvas are erected as an aid to meditation. Monasteries also include large libraries where the many texts and scriptures of the religion are stored. Finally there is a dharma hall where monks preach to the laity.

The traditional life of the monastery is intended to provide a suitable setting for monks and nuns to pursue the goal of enlightenment. The members of the sangha rise very early and devote themselves to meditation. In many traditions, at the appropriate time, members of the monastic community may leave the monastery to collect alms, sometimes chanting hymns or ringing a gong to attract attention to their begging. In the Theravada tradition the meal at the monastery is taken before noon as the only meal of the day.

TEACHING AND OTHER DUTIES

As well as visiting temples to offer devotion and prayer, members of the laity gather to hear sermons from the monks and ask questions. Memorizing, preserving, and teaching the dharma is the greatest service a monk can perform for others. Some preach in public places or before small gatherings in homes. The laity often place food and flowers before the chair of the Buddhist preacher.

Buddhist Theravada monks and novices collecting food on their daily alms round in Myanmar. Offering food is a way for lay people to accumulate merit. Besides food, laypersons will also offer the monastic community flowers, incense, and donations for books or printing religious literature. Financial help will also be given toward the running costs of the monastery and increasingly to support community work such as health, environmental, or education projects.

In Theravada countries, there are "observance days" or *uposatha* on the days of the quarter moon, new moon, and full moon. These are days of more intensive meditation and reflection. It is also an opportunity for laypersons to make special offerings or listen to the dharma from the monks. On new moon and full moon days, the senior monk in the sangha hall asks the other resident monks to declare openly their faults and misdeeds. Any monk who knows he is guilty and remains silent is committing a voluntary falsehood, violating the rule of the sangha. Very rarely, and only for specified serious offenses, a monk may be expelled from the sangha.

By custom he should not preach until he has been requested three times but then will teach anyone who sincerely asks. Until recently, particularly in Theravada countries, the monks were the main Buddhist teachers.

In the early evening monks often assemble in the sangha hall to read aloud from the scriptures and discuss their own spiritual concerns. Monasteries are not organized as a spiritual hierarchy. Any important decisions must be agreed on unanimously. Nor do the monks pledge obedience, as in Christian monasteries. In practice, however, certain monks are assigned specific duties that involve authority. Some for example are in charge of teaching the novices, others supervise the monastery garden, and so forth. An older monk is usually accepted as the leader of the group or abbot of the monastery.

DIFFERENT FORMS AND PRACTICES

Most Buddhist monasteries today follow similar practices to the ones that have been described here. However, just as the practice of the religion has developed many different forms, so has the life of the sangha. Because the laity can gain merit by donating food, cloth, money, and other gifts to the monastery, the daily needs of the monks are provided without the necessity of begging with a bowl. Even so the practice has survived as a symbol of the monk's withdrawal from ordinary life. Some sangha communities do not eat flesh or fish; others will accept them if the animal was not killed on their behalf. Monks are also permitted to accept invitations to meals at the homes of laypersons.

Stricter traditions also survive, sometimes in protest against the more liberal, worldly customs of the sangha in urban areas.

Women in Seoul, South Korea, parade through the streets with lanterns to celebrate the Buddha's birthday on the eighth day of the fourth lunar month of the year. The celebrations carry on well into the evening, lighting up the streets.

In Sri Lanka "forest monks" retreat into the remote areas of the country to live in caves or tents, meditating on the dharma. They attract pilgrims who make long journeys to give them alms and listen to their sermons. Other sangha communities are very recent. A community of 60 young monks at the 18th-century monastery of Amarbayasgalant in Mongolia, less than 80 miles from the Russian border, is attempting to reestablish Buddhist monastic culture from scratch after the religion was suppressed by Soviet Communists in 1938.

The Buddhist sangha has adapted to the modern world. Greater emphasis is given to practical social reform. The laity are encouraged to forego giving alms and instead are invited to support the sangha's establishment of schools, hospitals, and shelters for the homeless. Buddhist sanghas have joined international organizations, which meet to discuss contemporary issues such as nuclear disarmament, international justice, and human rights.

CHAPTER 8

BUDDHISM TODAY

As we enter the 21st century Buddhists are exploring the ways that their tradition relates to the changing social, cultural, and political situations in the world around them. They are far more culturally and nationally diverse than ever before. Just 100 years ago Buddhism was still mainly centered in its Asian birthplace. Today it reaches around the world.

In recent years Buddhists have become more socially engaged. Buddhists work actively with the poor, the homeless, the addicted, the dying, and those in prison. In San Francisco Buddhists run a major AIDS counseling service. Buddhists in New York teach classes in the Tibetan language and culture to children of Tibetan refugees. In Taiwan Buddhist organizations build hospitals and contribute to disaster relief. Around the world Buddhists have become more politically aware. They campaign against nuclear weapons, the arms trade, and the destruction of the environment.

A statue of the Buddha entering *parinirvana* in Wat Pho, the Temple of the Reclining Buddha, in Bangkok, Thailand. This statue, measuring almost 151 feet (46 meters) long and more than 49 feet (15 meters) high, was made in 1832; the temple itself dates back to 1688.

Buddhist scholars continue to examine the Buddhist teachings in light of modern-day problems such as human rights and medical ethics. They work to provide followers with guidelines for living an upright life.

SUPPRESSION AND REVIVAL IN ASIA

In the 16th century the first European traders arrived in Sri Lanka. With their arrival Buddhist countries encountered European culture. Europeans soon colonized countries such as Sri Lanka (then called Ceylon), Myanmar (then called Burma), Laos, Cambodia, and Vietnam. Christian missionaries followed and began to gain converts. Where Theravada Buddhism had once flourished, it began to falter.

In the 19th century a growing sense of nationalism began to sweep through southern Asia. In many countries nationalism led to a strengthening of Buddhism. The Buddhist revival began in Thailand (then called Siam), which Europeans had never colonized. King Rama IV (r. 1851–68) had been a Buddhist monk before becoming king. He instigated reforms in the sangha and began to modernize his country. Similar efforts were taking place elsewhere. In Myanmar King Mindon (r. 1853–78) made Buddhist revival a goal. In Sri Lanka in 1873 Buddhists invited a Methodist minister and a Buddhist monk to debate the merits of the two religions. The Buddhist won and newspapers around the world reported the event, creating new enthusiasm for the Buddhist faith. In 1892 Anagarika Dharmapala, a Sri Lankan, founded the first international Buddhist organization, the Mahabodhi Society. One of its goals was to unite all Buddhists.

The efforts to revitalize the sangha in southern Asia were largely successful. Traditional Theravada Buddhism remains the dominant religion in Sri Lanka, Myanmar, Cambodia, Laos, and Thailand.

LAOS AND CAMBODIA

The rise of communist regimes in Laos and Cambodia after 1975 meant disaster for Buddhism there. In Laos the government curtailed the activities of the sangha but did not carry out active persecution of the religion. The Khmer Rouge in Cambodia, however, tried to stamp out the religion entirely. The regime slaughtered monks and nuns and destroyed the sangha. Of probably 65,000 monks Cambodia lost all but about 3,000—a whole generation of its most highly educated people. Buddhism has begun to flourish again and the number of monks is now around 60,000. However, the people who would have passed on the traditions of the faith and learning are largely gone, since a generation of teachers was eradicated and religious training has been affected as a result.

KOREA

Korea was never colonized by or used as a base for Europeans. The Koreans themselves invited Catholic priests from China and a number converted to Christianity. However this first wave of Christians was violently suppressed by the Confucian regime in the late-19th century and Christianity more or less died out. It reappeared in force after World War II (1939–45), largely led by American Protestant missions. Buddhism was also marginalized by the Confucian regime, but not destroyed. Since the war it has lost some of its standing and support to Christianity, but monasteries and nunneries continue to flourish.

PERSECUTION IN CHINA

In China Buddhism suffered one of the worst periods of persecution in its history as a result of the collapse of the old imperial order after the 1911 revolution brought in a secular republic, and then, most intensely, under the rule of communism. From the 1950s onward Buddhism was restricted along with all other religions. During the horrific period of the Cultural Revolution (1966–75) Buddhism was pushed almost to the edge of survival as monasteries and temples were closed down, destroyed, or converted into factories; statues of the Buddha were smashed, melted down, or simply thrown away; and sacred texts were burned. Tens of thousands of Buddhist monks and nuns were persecuted and killed.

Since the early 1980s Buddhism, along with all the major faiths in China, can be practiced openly. Hundreds of monasteries and thousands of temples have been restored or rebuilt and the Buddhist sangha is once again a significant force within China.

RESTRICTIONS IN VIETNAM

Vietnam, colonized by the French, developed a strong minority of Catholics. In North Vietnam all religion suffered under the Communists, but Buddhism remained entrenched in the culture. In South Vietnam Buddhist monks, some of whom burned themselves to death in protest, demonstrated and remonstrated about the corruption of the South Vietnamese government and its ally, the United States. With the victory of the North over the South and the United States in 1976, Buddhism was severely restricted. Life for Buddhists has become easier in recent decades, though there are still restrictions and problems. Today it is estimated that 70 percent of Vietnamese are Buddhist.

GROWTH IN JAPAN

In the early 17th century the Japanese became alarmed at what they considered foreign tampering with Japanese affairs. Japan expelled the Christian missionaries, martyred many Japanese Christians, and closed its ports to almost all foreigners. Soon afterward all Japanese were forbidden to leave Japan. The country was effectively shut off from the rest of the world for the next 200 years. In the mid-19th century Japan reopened its ports and embraced Western technology. It soon developed into a world power. Although Japan's official religion was Shinto, its various forms of Mahayana Buddhism continued to thrive as a vital force in the life of its people.

Since the end of World War II the Japanese sangha has worked to draw laypersons into active participation in the religion. Young people's groups, public lectures and discussion classes, and social gatherings are part of the Japanese Buddhist revival. Though newer forms of Buddhism have attracted many followers, the ancient sects still thrive. Japanese Buddhists have played

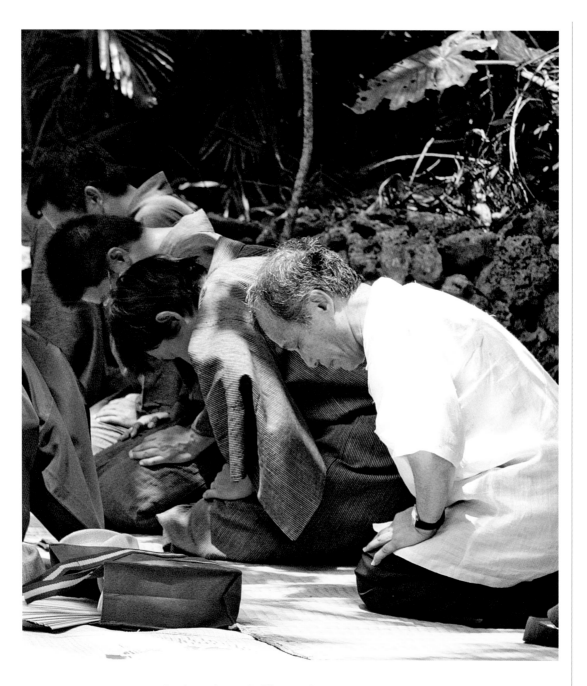

People worship at a Buddhist temple on Taketomi Island near
Okinawa in Japan. The temple has been run by a nun and
her husband, a monk. In Japan, women have for many years
played an important part in maintaining
Buddhist teaching and practice.

an active part in bringing different forms of Buddhism, especially Zen, to Europe and the United States.

BUDDHISM RETURNS TO MONGOLIA

Mongolians had practiced Buddhism since the 16th century. When the communists came into power they banned all practice of religion. During the 1930s more than 20,000 monks were executed and 800 monasteries destroyed. A few surviving monks kept the religion alive by meeting in secret.

In 1990 full religious freedom returned to Mongolia. Monks and nuns, now elderly, returned to the temples that were left. In the capital, Ulaanbaatar, the Gandan monastery had been turned into a museum. It is now a temple again, filled with laypersons as well as chanting monks and nuns. Monasteries built in the 16th and 18th centuries are now being restored. There has also been a big increase in the number of Mongolian young people who are becoming monks and nuns. Buddhist schools teach philosophy, logic, and language as well as the music and dance that is used in Buddhist ceremonies. Mongolian Buddhist art and sculpture are also being revived using classic materials and techniques.

THE TRAGEDY OF TIBET

For nearly 400 years Tibet has been ruled by Buddhist monks, with the Dalai Lama as its secular and religious leader. Tibetans believed him to be a reincarnation of the Bodhisattva Avalokitesvara. In 1950 China invaded Tibet. Two years later China annexed this smaller country and divided Tibet roughly in half, making each half into Chinese provinces.

Rongbuk Tibetan Buddhist monastery, the highest monastery in the world at 16,700 feet (5,060 meters). In the distance is the north face of Mount Everest. The monastery was built in 1899 but destroyed during China's Cultural Revolution. Prior to its destruction there were more than 500 monks and nuns. The monastery and nunnery have since been restored and a smaller Buddhist community has been reestablished here.

The current Dalai Lama, born in 1935, is the 14th in a line that stretches back more than 640 years. Buddhist priests selected him to be their next leader when he was two years old. They raised and educated him. In 1950, at the age of 15, he became the ruler of Tibet.

SUPPRESSION AND IMPRISONMENT

For nine years the young ruler tried to negotiate with the Chinese. The Chinese, for their part, said they were freeing the Tibetan people from the harsh rule of the Buddhist monks. In 1959, around the city of Lhasa, people rose up against the Chinese. In putting down the uprising Chinese troops killed as many as 87,000 Tibetan citizens. The Dalai Lama, then 24 years old, fled across the Himalayas to Dharamsala, India. He has lived there in exile ever since.

In the early years of the Chinese occupation, more than 1.2 million Tibetans died. The Chinese destroyed more than 6,200 monasteries. They imprisoned monks and nuns. They took the Buddhist treasures—jewels, gold, silver, statues, and holy items—back to China and sold them. They also placed many objects in museums, often designed to show how terrible life was under Buddhist rule. As the restrictions on religion in Tibet have eased, some of these objects have been returned to monasteries. Today it is possible to practice Buddhism quite freely as long as the image of the Dalai Lama is not displayed or anti-Chinese propaganda disseminated.

ELECTION OF RELIGIOUS LEADERS

In 1995, the Dalai Lama chose a six-year-old boy to be the next Panchen Lama, the second-highest religious figure in Tibetan Buddhism. The Chinese government rejected the Dalai Lama's choice and installed another boy instead. By interfering in the selection of the Panchen Lama, they hope to control the future of Tibetan religion.

In 1999 the 15-year-old boy whom the senior Tibetan lamas of the Kagyu School—one of the main schools of Tibetan Buddhism, along with Gelugpa, Nyingma, and Sakya—had chosen as Karmapa, another high-ranking religious figure, escaped from Tibet. The Chinese had previously accepted this young man. They now say he was not properly chosen and have found another person whom they claim is the true Karmapa.

The Dalai Lama now maintains a government-in-exile in Dharamsala. India permits him and his followers to govern themselves as long as they abide by India's laws. In 1989 the Dalai Lama won the Nobel Peace Prize for his nonviolent efforts to free his country. He has traveled around the world visiting world religious and political leaders.

RELIGIOUS PRACTICE IN TIBET

Since the 1980s monasteries in Tibet, as in China as a whole, have been extensively rebuilt and continue to function, albeit with limited populations of monks and nuns who are paid a government stipend. In recent years monks and nuns have restarted the tradition of long-term meditation retreats. Buddhist books and learning materials are published widely, including rare editions of texts thought to have been lost. Likewise lay Buddhists are free to practice their religion openly. Any political dissent among monastics, however, is fiercely repressed and punished.

BUDDHISM MOVES WEST

In the 19th century British, German, and French scholars began to translate some of the Buddhist scriptures into European languages. Some Europeans found in them new wisdom and a new perspective. During the 20th century Buddhism was established in most of western Europe. It became a presence not only in France, Germany, and the United Kingdom but also in Austria, Switzerland, the Netherlands, Belgium, Italy, Hungary, Poland, Scandinavia, Spain, and Greece.

In eastern Europe Tibetan Buddhism had come to Russia from Mongolia in the 17th century. It had been an officially recognized religion there since the 1700s. With the rise of communism the religion fell on hard times. Monasteries were destroyed or turned into public buildings. Today Buddhism is once again on the rise in the former Soviet Union. The ruined monasteries are being restored and new ones are being built.

People listen to a sermon from a Buddhist monk who preaches the teachings of Buddha in their new temple in Hampton, Minnesota.

BUDDHISM COMES TO AMERICA

In the mid-1800s a group of New England writers became interested in the thought and philosophy of Asia. They believed that there was an aspect of reality that transcended, or rose above, everyday life, and so they were called transcendentalists. One member of the group was Henry David Thoreau, who wrote *Walden*. This book describes the years he spent living in a one-room cabin on the banks of a Massachusetts pond and observing nature. Thoreau, like many of the transcendentalists, studied Asian thought and belief. He translated the Lotus Sutra from a French version into English. Thoreau never embraced Buddhism directly, but his mystical writings laid the ground for interest among intellectuals in Buddhism. Meanwhile Buddhism itself was entering the United States on the West Coast.

The California gold rush of 1849 attracted Chinese prospectors from across the Pacific Ocean. A few years later laborers from China helped build the transcontinental railroad. Chinese immigrants tended to live and work together in communities called Chinatowns, where they built Buddhist temples. Most of these early immigrants were members of the Pure Land Sect, which had developed in China.

Soon after, the first Japanese contract workers came to work on the plantations of Hawaii after the islands had been annexed by the United States. These immigrants were also primarily of the Pure Land branch of Buddhism. The Pure Land tradition continued and it is today part of the Buddhist traditions of America and of Canada. In Hawaii it was the beginning of a tradition that would make Buddhism the majority religion of the 50th state.

BUDDHISM IN THE AMERICAN HEARTLAND

In 1893 Buddhism came to the American heartland. Chicago hosted the Columbian Exposition that celebrated the progress

THE INFLUENCE OF D. T. SUZUKI

At the invitation of his Zen master the young D. T. Suzuki made arrangements to go to Illinois as a translator of Buddhist texts. In his last meditation session in Kamakura in Japan, he managed, in his words, to "break through"—meaning that he had achieved a higher degree of insight. He was spiritually prepared for his work in the United States.

D. T. Suzuki's work had a great influence. He spent 11 years translating Buddhist texts and Japanese commentaries that attracted a wide readership. Later, in the 1950s, he returned to the United States to teach at Columbia University and other schools. His lectures on Buddhism in general and Zen in particular attracted enthusiastic audiences. Millions read his books, such as *Introduction to Zen Buddhism*, *Living by Zen*, and *The Essentials of Zen Buddhism*.

of science and technology in the United States. The organizers decided to recognize the spiritual side of humanity as well and organized a World Parliament of Religions. Among the Buddhists who attended were Anagarika Dharmapala and a Zen master named Soyen Shaku.

At the parliament Soyen Shaku met a religious publisher who was looking for a translator. The Zen master recommended a young student who had some knowledge of English. The student was Daisetz Teitaro Suzuki, who would become better known as D. T. Suzuki (1870–1966) and would popularize Zen in the United States so that it became a household word.

THE APPEAL OF ZEN BUDDHISM

Why was Zen Buddhism so appealing to Americans? Perhaps for the same reason that it had been in Asia: It put forth the message that people should make the most out of their existence through self-discipline, meditation, and instruction and thus find fulfillment in life. Zen teaches one to live in the present, a view that many Americans share. For the Zen Buddhist the quality of experience here and now assumes paramount importance. Zen enlightenment consists of the discovery of the profound meaning of day-to-day experience. This was a way of life that could be accepted even while keeping one's own religion.

Zen entered American literature through the writings of the "beat" authors of the 1950s, especially Jack Kerouac and Allen Ginsberg. The term *beat author* described writers who broke the conformity of the decade, and used passion and raw emotion as sources of inspiration in their work. They used the idea of tangential thinking, plots that did not have a real progression, and characters who were not

CULTURAL DIFFERENCES

A clear division still remains between American-born Buddhists and their Asian-born counterparts. Both practice forms of the same religion but from widely differing cultural perspectives. American Buddhists tend to focus on meditation and its techniques. Laypersons, particularly women, play an important role. The Asian Buddhist experience, rooted in hundreds or thousands of years of tradition and culture, is more conservative. Moreover American Buddhism has been slow to develop a monastic tradition, the mainstay of much Asian Buddhism. For the most part the two groups do not mix, yet each recognizes the other's devotion to the same path.

really characters to highlight their breaking with conformity. Today Zen meditation centers are found throughout the United States. Zen Buddhism claims more than 9 million adherents worldwide.

Many Buddhist traditions can now be found in the United States. New religious movements based on Buddhism have come from Japan, often using unconventional conversion methods and practicing forms of Buddhism not necessarily supported by their country of origin. Tibetan Buddhism has become very popular through the figure of the Dalai Lama, the conversion of some high-profile stars such as Richard Gere, and the popular writings of lamas such as Chogyam Trungpa. His books on living and dying have opened up for discussion taboo areas such as death and provided many people with a sense of being guided through life.

Meditiation centers can be found in any medium-sized town, and many Buddhist terms, ideas, and practices have now become commonplace within both mainstream medicine and in the burgeoning alternative health world. Buddhist magazines such as *Tricycle* and *Shambhala Sun* are available on newsstands, and Buddhism shapes the work and thinking of leading activists such as the eco-philosopher Joanna Macy and poets such as Gary Snyder. Buddhism is now part of the backdrop of contemporary America.

For many people Buddhism is not so much a religion as a tool. The Dalai Lama has said he is not interested in conversions to Buddhism. He wants people to become better Christians or Jews, or whatever their original faith background is. For many Buddhism is a philosophy that informs their lives, rather than a faith by which they live.

BUDDHISM AND THE FUTURE

In 1950 the World Fellowship of Buddhists (WFB) was organized to foster fellowship among the many different schools of Buddhism and to spread the faith. Today the WFB has 140 regional centers in more than 40 countries, serving most of the world's

Buddhist scholars (below) including the Dalai Lama met in Barcelona, Spain, in September 2007 to attend a conference on "The Art of Happiness." The Dalai Lama opened the Tibet House Foundation in Barcelona, met members of the Tibetan Buddhist community, and held meetings with other religious groups to further interfaith dialogue.

350 million Buddhists. In the year 2000 it celebrated its 50th anniversary by opening the World Buddhist University, a university without walls in Bangkok, Thailand. This school offers education and training in different parts of the world through a network of Buddhist institutions and scholars.

The WFB works to increase awareness of Buddhism. In 1999 the United Nations formally recognized the day celebrated throughout the Buddhist world as the anniversary of the birth, enlightenment, and *parinirvana* of the Buddha, thus realizing one of the WFB's important goals.

Buddhism offers many benefits for the modern world. Modern interpretations of the Buddha's life and teachings have underscored his humanity and his rational approach to the problems of human suffering. Many Buddhist scholars have stressed the relevance of Buddhist teachings to present-day social and ethical issues. The Buddhist teaching of a kinship of all living things is particularly appealing in a world faced with environmental problems. Buddhists claim that their religion can be the basis for a truly democratic society and even for world peace.

The Buddhist emphasis on compassion and wisdom provides high ideals for any society. Whether one leads a religious or a nonreligious life, the teachings of the Buddha make one think and encourage a life of concern for others.

In his Nobel Prize acceptance speech in Oslo, Norway, on December 10, 1989, the Dalai Lama quoted a traditional prayer. It summarizes the high ideals of Buddhism:

"For as long as space endures,
And for as long as living beings remain,
Until then may I, too, abide
To dispel the misery of the world."

FACT FILE

Worldwide Numbers
The Buddhist faith is 2,500 years old and has some 370 million followers worldwide.

Holy Symbol
The Buddhist holy symbol is that of a wheel with eight spokes, which is said to represent the Eightfold Path to enlightenment.

Holy Writings
The Tipitaka (Pali version used by Theravada Buddhism) and Tripitaka (Sanskrit version used by Mahayana Buddhists) means "three baskets" and contains the discourses of the Buddha, rules for monks and nuns, and further knowledge.

Holy Places
Each Buddhist country has its own pilgrimage sites. In India, sites in the north of the country that hold relevance to the Buddha are seen as important to all Buddhists.

Founders
The Buddhist faith arose from a prince, Siddhartha Gautama, who came to understand suffering and how to end it. It was after this that he was given the title of Buddha, the enlightened one. Buddhists follow the teachings of the Buddha.

Festivals
The dates, nature, and names of Buddhist festivals vary with the tradition, customs, and culture of the country. Celebrations are generally linked to events in the Buddha's life or events in Buddhist history. They involve people visiting a temple, bringing offerings of incense, cloth, flowers, and money. Most festivals follow a lunar calendar.

BIBLIOGRAPHY

Alphonso-Karkala, John B. *An Anthology of Indian Literature.* New Delhi: Indian Council for Cultural Relations, 1987.

Conze, Edward, ed. *Buddhist Texts through the Ages.* New York: Harper & Row, 1964.

Dalai Lama. *An Open Heart.* Boston, Mass.: Little Brown, 2001.

Dalai Lama. *Freedom in Exile: The Autobiography of His Holiness the Dalai Lama of Tibet.* London: Abacus, 1998.

De Bary, Theodore. *The Buddhist Tradition in India, China, and Japan.* New York: Random House, 1969.

Hagen, Steve. *Buddhism Plain and Simple.* New York: Broadway Books, 1997.

O'Brien, Joanne, Martin Palmer, David B. Barrett, and Joanne O'Brien. *The Atlas of Religion.* Berkeley, Calif.: University of California Press, 2007.

FURTHER READING

Batchelor, Stephen. *The Awakening of the West: The Encounter of Buddhism and Western Culture.* Berkeley, Calif.: Parallax Press, 1994.

Breuilly, Elizabeth, Joanne O'Brien, Martin Palmer, and Martin E. Marty. *Religions of the World: The Illustrated Guide to Origins, Beliefs, Traditions & Festivals, Revised Edition.* New York: Checkmark Books, 2005.

Dalai Lama. *The Compassionate Life.* Boston, Mass.: Wisdom Publications, 2003.

Fontana, David. *Discover Zen: A Practical Guide to Personal Serenity.* San Francisco: Chronicle Books, 2001.

Ikeda, Daisaku. *Buddhism Day by Day: Wisdom for Modern Life.* Santa Monica, Calif.: Middleway Press, 2006.

Khyentse, Jamyang. *What Makes You Not a Buddhist.* Boston, Mass.: Shambhala, 2008.

Maguire, Jack. *Essential Buddhism: A Complete Guide to Beliefs and Practices.* New York: Pocket Books, 2001.

Murcott, Susan. *The First Buddhist Women.* Berkeley, Calif.: Parallax Press, 1991.

Napthali, Sarah. *Buddhism for Mothers of Young Children.* Crows Nest, NSW, Australia: Allen & Unwin, 2008.

Prebish, Charles S. *Historical Dictionary of Buddhism.* Historical dictionaries of religions, philosophies, and movements, no. 1. Metuchen, N.J.: Scarecrow Press, 1993.

Smith, Huston, and Philip Novak. *Buddhism: A Concise Introduction.* New York: HarperCollins, 2005.

Sivaraksa, Sulak. *Conflict, Culture, Change: Engaged Buddhism in a Globalizing World.* Boston, Mass.: Wisdom Publications, 2005.

Vajragupta. *Buddhism: Tools for Living Your Life.* Birmingham, U.K.: Windhorse Publications, 2007.

WEB SITES

Further facts and figures, history, and current status of the religion can be found on the following Web sites:

www.bbc.co.uk/religion/religions/buddhism
A comprehensive guide to Buddhism.

www.aboutbuddhism.org
Information giving a basic understanding of Buddhism as an ancient religion and philosophy.

www.religioustolerance.org/buddhism
An outline of Buddhist beliefs and practices.

www.urbandharma.org
Buddhism in America.

buddhism.about.com
Origins, history, and basic doctrines of the faith.

GLOSSARY

ahimsa—The noninjury of living beings.

alms—In Buddhism, the offering of food to monks on their daily rounds, and the donation of goods and money to the monasteries.

Amitabha or Amida—The bodhisattva whose name means "Buddha of Boundless Light" and who dwells in the paradise called the Pure Land.

arhat—A Buddhist monk who is free from all illusions and who has achieved personal enlightenment.

Avalokitesvara—The bodhisattva who looks on his devotees with compassion and love. The most popular bodhisattva.

bardo—A human soul between the stages of after-death and rebirth.

bhikkhu—A fully ordained monk who has left his home and renounced all his possessions in order to follow the Way of the Buddha.

Bodhi tree—The bo (fig) tree beneath which the meditating Siddhartha Gautama sat before he achieved enlightenment.

Bodhidharma—The legendary monk who brought Buddhism from India to China in the sixth century C.E.

bodhisattva—A being in the final stages of attaining buddhahood, who has vowed to help all sentient beings achieve nirvana, or enlightenment, before he himself achieves it.

Buddha—The "Enlightened One."

Buddha nature—The nature innate in every sentient being. The potential for attaining buddhahood.

chaitya—An assembly hall for monks.

dharma—The ultimate law, or doctrine, as taught by Buddha, which consists of the Four Noble Truths and the Eightfold Path.

dhyana—A state of mind achieved through higher meditation.

Hinayana—Literally, "small vehicle." A term used by the Mahayanists to describe earlier orthodox sects of Buddhism (Theravada School).

Their scriptures are written in Pali, an ancient Indian language. *See also* THERAVADA

karma—Literally, "deed." A concept that binds its followers to an endless cycle of birth, death, and rebirth and, according to one's deeds in life, determines the condition of one's rebirth.

koan (*gong'an*)—A riddle, tale, or short statement used by Zen masters to bring their students to sudden insight.

lama—Literally, "superior one." A Buddhist monk or teacher of Tibet.

Mahayana—Literally, "great vehicle." One of the two major forms of Buddhism, Mahayana is considered the more liberal and practical. Its scriptures are written in Sanskrit. *See also* THERAVADA

Maitreya—Literally, "Friendly One." The bodhisattva who embodies the virtues of compassion and benevolence.

Manjushri—Literally, "Beautiful Auspicious One." The bodhisattva who embodies the virtues of wisdom and eloquence.

mantra—Ritual sound, word, or phrase used to evoke a certain religious effect.

Mara—The personification of evil. The god of death.

nirvana—Literally, "extinction." The ultimate goal of Buddhists, characterized as the extinction of both craving and the separate ego. The state of peace and quietude attained by extinguishing all illusions.

parinirvana—Death of the Buddha.

samsara—The continuous cycle of birth, death, and rebirth.

sangha—An organized assembly of Buddhist monks.

stupa—A dome, or pagoda, in which sacred relics are deposited.

sutra (sutta)—Literally, "thread" or "string." A scripture containing the teachings of the Buddha.

Theravada—Literally, "School of the Elders." Also known as HINAYANA. One of the two major forms of Buddhism, Theravada is considered to be the original and orthodox form of Buddhism.

Tipitaka or Tripitaka—Literally, "three baskets." According to Buddhist belief the scriptures were stored in three baskets, dividing the Buddha's teachings into the code of discipline for monks, his sermons and discourses, and the higher doctrine (Buddhist philosophy and psychology).

urna—A mark on the Buddha's forehead, between his eyebrows, that signifies his great intuition.

ushanisha—A protuberance atop Buddha's head that signifies his great wisdom.

vihara—Cave dwellings for the monks.

Zen or Chan—Forms of Mahayana Buddhism in Japan and China, respectively.

INDEX

ABOUT THE AUTHOR

Madhu Bazaz Wangu has taught at the University of Pittsburgh, where she earned a Ph.D. in religious studies. She is the winner of several awards for her work as a freelance artist and has also taught classes in the Hindi language.

ABOUT THE SERIES EDITORS

Martin Palmer is the founder of ICOREC (International Consultancy on Religion, Education, and Culture) in 1983 and is the secretary-general of the Alliance of Religions and Conservation (ARC). He is the author of many books on world religions.

Joanne O'Brien has an M.A. degree in Theology and has written a range of educational and general reference books on religion and contemporary culture. She is co-author, with Martin Palmer and Elizabeth Breuilly, of *Religions of the World* and *Festivals of the World* published by Facts On File Inc.

PICTURE CREDITS